Purposefully Prepared to Persevere

EDDIE CONNOR

Bloomington, IN · authorHOUSE · Milton Keynes, UK

AuthorHouse™
1663 Liberty Drive, Suite 200
Bloomington, IN 47403
www.authorhouse.com
Phone: 1-800-839-8640

AuthorHouse™ *UK Ltd.*
500 Avebury Boulevard
Central Milton Keynes, MK9 2BE
www.authorhouse.co.uk
Phone: 08001974150

© 2006 Eddie Connor. All rights reserved.

No part of this book may be reproduced, stored in a retrieval system, or transmitted by any means without the written permission of the author.

First published by AuthorHouse 4/18/2006

ISBN: 1-4259-1057-2 (sc)

Library of Congress Control Number: 2005911254

Printed in the United States of America
Bloomington, Indiana

This book is printed on acid-free paper.

All scriptures references are from the King James Version, New King James Version, and New International Version Bible.

CONTENTS

Acknowledgements vii
About the Author ix
Preface xiii
Chapter One Destined to Overcome the Odds 1
Chapter Two "2" Extraordinary "2" Be Ordinary 25
Chapter Three Power Perfected through Pain 37
Chapter Four You Are God's Masterpiece 49
Chapter Five I Won't Give Up 57
Chapter Six My Mind Is on a Mission 64
Chapter Seven You Are a Restorer of the Brethren 73
Chapter Eight Where Is Your Roar? 85
Chapter Nine You Are a Statue of Liberty 93
The Reclamation of a Nation 100

ACKNOWLEDGEMENTS

Dedicated to my Mother, Dr. Janice Connor. Thank you for your inspiration and continual love throughout the years.

You are a blessing to me.

Love,
Eddie

†

ABOUT THE AUTHOR

Eddie Connor, born April 7, 1982, resides in Oak Park, Michigan but grew up in Kingston, Jamaica. His mother, Dr. Janice Connor has been a missionary to Jamaica for the past eighteen years, yet has raised Eddie and his brother Elijah to be standout men of excellence. Upon spending the early years of his life in Jamaica, Eddie affirms that his thirst for knowledge can be attributed to the British education he received in the exotic island. On his travels back to the United States, Eddie recognized the call of God on his life at the age of twelve. Growing up in the metropolitan area of Detroit, Eddie excelled in academics, sports, and the overall structure of life. Yet, betwixt his Jamaican and U.S. roots Eddie could attest to the fact even at a young age, that he was different. A product of a single parent household, along with his brother, Eddie realizes that he wasn't born with a "silver spoon" in his mouth, but was raised by a strong mother, who instilled in him life-long values and the importance of governing himself as a positive individual. These daily lessons in life prepared Eddie, for the biggest challenge of his life.

Eddie's greatest test came at the age of fifteen, on January 1, 1998, when he was diagnosed with Cancer. Eddie preached his first message a few months later after the diagnosis at the age of fifteen in Kingston, Jamaica proclaiming from Psalm 118:17,

"I shall not die, but live and declare the works of the Lord." Eddie Connor affirms that he was Destined to Overcome the Odds. He discovered in the midst of chemotherapy treatments, radiation, nausea, hair loss, surgery, psychological, and emotional debilitating circumstances how to reach within the abyss of his soul and Resurrect Faith, Resurrect Determination, Resurrect positive thoughts, Resurrect a smile in the midst of sadness, and even Resurrect the notion of overcoming the odds. Reverend Eddie Connor is declaring the works of the Lord and the healing power of God has touched this young man's life, as he has miraculously been healed from Cancer. Reverend Connor is a graduate of Eastern Michigan University, having earned a Bachelor of Science in Secondary Education with a focus in History. He is also a spokesman for the American Cancer Society.

Reverend Eddie Connor is currently a teacher at Ferndale University High School, in Ferndale, Michigan. Reverend Connor influences the various sectors of academia and his surrounding community as an Evangelist, Licensed/Ordained Reverend, Youth Pastor, Teacher, Academic Assistant, Resident Advisor, Youth Counselor, First Year Student Mentor, Dr. Martin Luther King, Jr./Caesar Chavez/Rosa Parks (KCP) college days program counselor, and Summer Incentive Program (SIP) counselor. Reverend Connor has garnered a plethora of awards and honors such as 2001-2002 Dean's List Award recipient, 2003 NAACP Male Student of the Year Award recipient, 2003 Kappa Delta Pi educational honor society, 2004 Martin Luther King, Jr. Humanitarian Award recipient, 2004 Eastern Michigan University President for a Day, 2004 Eastern Michigan University Ambassador, 2004 Resident Advisor Leader of the Year award recipient, 2004 Eastern Michigan University Campus Leader of the Year award recipient, and 2004 Phi Alpha Theta educational honor society member.

God has truly given Eddie Connor a voice to reach individuals of all ages, races, and backgrounds in this day and time. A young man of passion, determination, and intellectual fortitude desires to impact minds in perilous times, by enhancing the lives of others and expressing the power to persevere, which will ultimately propel individuals beyond all obstacles.

PREFACE

The sole purpose of this book is written in order to impact minds in these perilous times of today. There is an ardent call that compels each and every one of us to advance beyond complacency and move to a higher level of purposeful living. Within the scope of my life I have traversed from hardship to healing, from pain to power, from the abyss of enslavement to the apex of freedom. These life lessons that were steeped in inner turmoil have produced an outward testimony in order to resurrect hope, determination, and love in your heart. Our world is facing grave difficulties and hardships on every side. Yet the strength that lies within you and I must be cultivated in order that we may enhance and bring life to the dark and desolate places of our world. To bring life and light to that which is dark it must first reside within us. We must seek to strengthen areas of weakness, redeem that which is lost, bring nobility to that which is ignoble, and ignite the flame of freedom and fortitude in the lives of those who surround us.

The strength of God that lies within will guide and mend the brokenhearted. This strength will restore America from the low alleys to its highest valleys from its small housetops to its grandiose hilltops. The strength that invigorates can regenerate and bring vitality to our lives.

We have often reached and never grasped the enormity of greatness and the ability to overcome in spite of hardships. Yet the pages and photos of your life are a testimony that you are a survivor and a symbol of perseverance. The maladies that have sought to overtake and debilitate our lives are only being used to transform our concept in order to regenerate and rehabilitate our purpose in life. As these pages unfold before your very eyes and hands, I pray that your eyes become enlightened and your hands feel the surge of God's healing, which will enrapture and penetrate your total being. As your insight and wisdom is increased, dispense the richness of esteeming value into the lives of others, whereby your life, neighborhood, community, state, nation, and entire world will be changed by the power that God has given you to persevere.

Chapter One

DESTINED TO OVERCOME THE ODDS

If you could just for a moment, think of your biggest fear. Is it poverty, relationship loss, failure, or even death? In whatever way the case presents itself, faith must prevail beyond fear. Fear minus Faith equals Failure. Have you ever been so low, so down and out that you felt like giving up? Has your psyche ever been in such a conundrum, that you felt life had become meaningless? Ponder about your life. Think about the point of where you are, where you've come from, and where you're going. Think about your highs and lows, the ups and downs, the apex of achievement, and the cave of calamity. As you look back at the yesterdays, maybe you can say that your Character has been Cultivated in Chaos, Power has been Perfected through Pain, Endurance brought about Ebullience, Ingenuity overcame Idiosyncratic behavior, and Faith overcame Fear.

The world we live in befuddles me from time to time. A strong emphasis is placed on what we have, rather than who we are. Take a stroll down some of the most elegant, grandiose, and sophisticated places on the planet and you will find that glamour outweighs gratitude. Our possessions are not more valuable than who we are. The best part of you is not your apparel, your palatial estate, your stunning physique, or the car you drive. For the best part of you cannot be seen with the naked eye. The outward possessions distinguish you from no one, but that which you possess from within, distinguishes you from all others. You are your most valuable possession. If you don't cultivate your character, your gifts, your talents, and your educational prowess then who will? Do you know who you are? What distinguishes you from the masses? What is your purpose on this planet?

These are just some of the questions I asked myself, after being diagnosed with Cancer on January 1, 1998, at the age of fifteen. Yes, the "Big C" word. I can remember the whole ordeal, as if it occurred yesterday. I had been dealing with some chest pains for the past few weeks, around Christmas time. However, being the fighter that I am, I tried to ignore the pain and persevere through it. I was running cross-country in high school, preparing myself for the upcoming basketball season, in order to be in top physical condition. The pain in the left area of my chest was on and off again. Yet, as the days progressed, I kept going in spite of how I felt. I was experiencing chest pains, but I didn't want to tell anybody, especially my mother because I knew she would worry. So, deep within my heart, in spite of the pain, I could only hope to feel better.

On January 1, 1998, my friend from Alabama was in town for a few days, and the Rose Bowl game between Michigan and Ohio State was a must see television event. So, I went over his house to watch the highly anticipated football game. That day I was feeling somewhat better, and the game helped me suppress the pain. However, during halftime of the game I was experiencing pain beyond belief. The pain felt, as if someone was stabbing me in my chest repeatedly. I told my friend, "Man, you've got to call your parents and get me to a hospital immediately, my chest is hurting." As he ran to the phone, I was trying to relax and breathe. Yet, each time I inhaled, my air supply shortened, making it very difficult to breathe. His parents contacted my mother and drove me home. My mother quickly helped me into the car and drove me to the hospital. Immediately, my mother began pleading the blood of Jesus over my life, and rebuking the enemy. My body, writhing in pain, was laid on the hospital bed, as my life flashed before my eyes.

I was just a teenager at fifteen years of age, lying on a hospital bed in awe of my circumstances. My dreams and aspirations of greatness seemed to be slipping away. It was difficult to even think beyond the pain that I endured. The doctors and nurses were entering and exiting my room, continually checking my vital signs, as I reclined on the bed in tearful pain. I can remember turning my head with the little energy I had, to look at my mother, and the greater pain I felt watching her intercede on my behalf. The doctors brought me their report on my condition and diagnosed me with a punctured lung. When I heard the news, I tried to believe that statement, but deep within, I knew it was a misdiagnosis.

Later, I was taken, by ambulance, to another hospital. By this time, the ability to breathe on my own was in jeopardy. Every time I tried to take a deep breath, I felt excruciating pain beyond belief. I was placed on a breathing respirator, as tubes were inserted throughout my body. As I thought to myself what is going on with me, I was thinking in my mind, "God, I really need you." Whatever I couldn't verbalize, I thought in my mind. I tell you the truth, the devil was after my life. John 10:10 declares, "The thief (devil) comes only to steal, kill, and to destroy: but I (Jesus) have come that you may have life, and have it more abundantly." The enemy was trying to steal my life, kill me, and destroy what God had destined for my life. As I lay on that hospital bed, I had to do some soul searching, like never before. Many tests and x-rays were performed on my body. The doctors informed me that the pain I experienced was due to my cells replicating abnormally quickly. My lymph nodes were also replicating too fast. As the doctor was informing me about the circumstances he said, "You have Cancer." Immediately my eyes widened and I thought to myself, "What in the world is going on?" I couldn't believe this was real, first chest pains, now Cancer. The doctor was trying to comfort me, but the damage was already done. I remember him saying, "We're going to have to perform surgery and give you radiation and chemotherapy treatments."

One statement that I can recall over the years is when the doctor told me, "Don't ask why me?" I initially thought to myself, "Who does this guy think he is to tell me what not to ask? You've already ruined my day by diagnosing me with a disease, now you want to tell me what not to ask?" He was talking, yet my mind was elsewhere.

All I could think about was being a teenager with Cancer and living another day. I thought about my dreams, my goals, and my life. Can you imagine being in my shoes, in the prime years of your teenage life, then getting the shock of your life by being told you have Cancer? I wanted to be every other healthy teenager but myself that day. Despite the doctor's wishes, I asked, "God, why me?" Yet, I didn't hear an answer.

The words of Jesus, as he hung on the cross, flashed before my mind, "My God, My God why have you forsaken me?" I cried an ocean's worth of tears that night, hoping that one day my sorrow would turn into joy and my life would be resurrected again. Upon the passing of days before my surgery, my mother was constantly interceding and playing healing tapes and scripture by my bedside. The Bible declares in Romans 10:17, "Faith comes by hearing and hearing by the Word of God." It's important for us to watch what we allow into our ear gates. If all you're hearing is doubt and unbelief, you will eventually become a by-product of what you hear. Faith produces Faith. These healing tapes and scriptures were Faith builders because it helped to eradicate the doubt, fear, and unbelief in my life.

My mother was my everything, as she was with me practically 24/7, praying, comforting me, telling me she loved me, anointing me, and rebuking the spirit of death over my life in the name of Jesus. She was also very protective of who came into my hospital room to see me.

Let me tell you, there are always those individuals who only want to see you when you're going through. They don't want anything to do with you, as long as you're looking clean, sharp, and sophisticated. But once you go through a little storm here they come, "I just want to see how you're doing," they say. They enjoy seeing you when you're down, in order to stimulate gossip and discourage you. However, the devil is a liar. You've got to get out of here. I don't need any whisperers or spectators, because I'd rather fight the devil with my mom and my God.

You don't need whisperers during the storms in your life, you need warriors. You need someone who will lift up the blood stained banner of the power of God, against the enemy and fight for you, as if they were fighting for themselves. The devil is real and he hates you, he wants to annihilate you, because you are a threat to him. The devil will use people, circumstances, diseases, or whatever else he can to destroy your life. Yet, you must remain steadfast, unmovable, and always abound in the work of the Lord, (I Corinthians 15:58).

As the days prolonged, my date for surgery was at hand. I can once again remember going into surgery, which was such a long ordeal. I was given a certain anesthetic, which produced severe hallucinations in my body. My grandparents and mother were by my side. I can remember as I was going into surgery, the devil told me I was going to die and wouldn't see my sixteenth birthday, which was a few months away. I was experiencing severe hallucinations and I even said to my mother, "I'm ready to die." I was saying, "I'm ready to go to heaven." She immediately said, "You shall live and not die and declare the works of the Lord, (Psalm 118:17)." My mother told me she loved me, encouraged me to fight, and told me I better not leave her. See, once again the enemy will try to work in any situation, especially when you are weak. That's why it's imperative to have people in your corner that will fight for you, when you can't fight for yourself.

My mother didn't have the time to go and grab a Bible, but she had the Word of God down in her heart. The psalmist declared, "Thy word have I hid in my heart that I might not sin against thee (Psalm 119:11)." The enemy will strategically try to catch you off guard, but you've got to put the Word of God on your situation. Apply the Word of God as a balm to the bruises, scars, and scrapes that life brings to you, and I'm a witness that God will provide healing for your infirmities. For "He (Jesus) was wounded for our transgressions, He was bruised for our iniquities, the chastisement of our peace was upon Him, and by His stripes we are healed (Isaiah 53:5)." As the hallucination subsided, I was given a weaker anesthetic for the surgery. When the surgery was completed, the "bad" cells were removed and a catheter was

Purposefully Prepared to Persevere 7

placed under my skin, so that I could receive radiation and chemotherapy treatment. I felt great after the surgery, yet I didn't want to receive radiation or chemotherapy. However, the doctor explained to me, I needed to have this treatment, in order to avoid any reoccurrence of Cancer cells spreading throughout my body.

After my three-week stay in the hospital, I was released to go home and get ready to start chemotherapy treatments. This was the beginning of my up-hill climb. In retrospect of my battle with Cancer, I never would say the words, "I have Cancer." Upon growing up in a Christian household, I was taught that death and life is in the power of the tongue, (Proverbs 18:21), so I knew that my words contained power. I can't stress the fact enough that your words are powerful. Your words are a creative force, that stimulate positive or negative results. If you go around saying, "I'm a failure," you will fail. Yet, if you continue to say, "I am more than a conqueror," then you will be more than a conqueror.

Refuse to be bound by negative words and become a person who is inundated with the way God thinks of you. You are more than a conqueror because greater is He (Jesus) that is in you than he (satan) that is in the world, (Rom. 8:37, I John 4:4). God has given us power through the Holy Spirit, and "Whatever we bind on earth will be bound in heaven and whatsoever we loose on earth it will be loosed in heaven (Matthew 16:19)."

Now is the time for you to bind up negativity, generational curses, diseases, financial instability, and every other malady in the name of Jesus. Then begin to loose prosperity in your finances, health, relationships, spirit, soul, body, and decree God's Word in your life, (III John 1:2). God has given you the power to, "Call things that be not as though they were (Romans 4:17)." So, when the enemy has been working and strategizing to defeat you in a certain area of your life, that's your time to proclaim in Jesus' name that you are victorious, declare that you shall not be defeated, because through Christ you can do all things, (Philippians 4:13). Right at that immediate time, things in the spirit realm have shifted. In the natural your situation still seems the same, but in the spirit realm, God is on the scene instructing you to walk by faith and not by sight. I can't see it, but I still believe that I'm victorious and shall overcome every obstacle.

You might not see the victory naturally, but spiritually God is showing you that the battle is already won. I've often thought to myself, "Why am I going through this ordeal?" Yet, I was reminded that God is not the author of sickness, "For every good and perfect gift comes from above (James 1:17)." Satan is the author of confusion, sickness, and disease.

We have heard people say, "God did this to you, it was God who took your beloved relative home with Him, because He wanted another beautiful flower in heaven." That's nonsense. I'm telling you that God doesn't curse you with sickness. Satan's occupation is to curse you. Yet, God's mode of operation is to bless you.

I'm reminded of the story of Job, a man who was richly blessed by God in all areas of his life while lacking nothing. So, satan approaches God with a proposal and declares, "The only reason Job serves you is because you give him everything he wants, you have to buy him, in order for him to serve you." Satan continues, "Let me take away everything you've given him, curse him, and see if Job will still serve you." God listens to the proposal and decides to let the devil do what he will, except take his life. Job endures hell on earth, his family members die, endures being stricken with boils, and he loses everything he owns (Job 1:1 - 2:13). Yet he still serves God.

My point here is that God will allow certain circumstances to occur in your life, in order to test your faith, "For the trying of your faith produces patience (James 1:2)." God won't put more on you than you can bear.

Jesus said to Mary at the tomb of Lazarus, "This sickness is not unto death, but for the glory of God, that the Son of God may be glorified through it (John 11:4)." What you're going through is just a test that will cultivate character, determination, and power within you.

As I began the up-hill climb of chemotherapy, I was going to the Cancer center on a daily basis. I remember experiencing nausea, fatigue, and many other side effects. One of the most painful experiences I faced, occurred when I stood in front of the bathroom mirror one night, and as I ran my fingers through my head I watched as clumps of my hair fell to the floor. It was as if I was watching my body disintegrate before my eyes. I yelled for my mother to come quickly, as I immediately broke down and cried. I would go to sleep at night and wake up with hair all over my pillow. I was so distraught, emotionally and psychologically broken. I began taking oral medication, while receiving radiation and chemotherapy, which led to increased weight gain. My countenance was virtually unrecognizable, from the young man I used to be. Since I was losing my hair, I decided to cut it all off, yet I hated having no hair on my head. Yet, like always my mother tried to cheer me up and help me to look on the bright side, and she would say, "You can now wear the bald haircut like your favorite athlete, Michael Jordan." To a certain degree, I tried to find solace in those words, but it didn't last long. I began to sink into a state of depression. I would look at other young people and wish to be like them. I shied away from the public sector because of my appearance. I wanted to lie in the bed and feel sorry for myself, and I didn't like myself at all. I began to form a negative self-concept of who I was. I would wear a hat low over my eyes, in utter shame and self-pity. I absolutely hated chemotherapy treatments. I would go to the Cancer center from three to five times per week. I was tired of the doctors, nurses, and everyone else in the center. I would leave the Cancer center nauseous and sickly, after receiving chemotherapy treatment.

My mother, who was the only constant figure in my life, continued to encourage and pray for me. She only allowed me to eat healthy meals, in order to fight off Cancer. I can recall eating an abundance of fruits and vegetables, whether I wanted to or not, because my Mother was trying to save my life. Some of the fruits and vegetables I ate consisted of cantaloupe, strawberries, blueberries, tomatoes, baked yams, green beans, mixed vegetables, and even beets (which I detest to this very day). I also drank plenty of cranberry and grape juice.

I had no choice but to eat foods that were high in nutritional value, because I went into the Cancer center for a weekly blood count, which checked my platelet level and cell count. I had to eat certain foods, which were aforementioned, in order to help my body fight when the radiation would destroy the cells. I encourage you, not to wait until your cholesterol is high or until you're afflicted with a disease to begin eating healthy, but start now.

The Bible reminds us that this body we live in is not our own but it is the temple of the Holy Ghost, (I Corinthians 6:19, 20). Its important that you put the proper foods into your body, because if you don't, it will break down. Just like a car needs to have its oil changed, its tires rotated, or air filter changed, so the body must be taken care of as well. However, if you don't or haven't been taking care of your body, going in for check ups, or scheduling an appointment with a doctor, then begin to do it. Some people avoid the doctor, because they're afraid of bad news. Yet, I encourage you to go to the doctor. You've got to be wise and be a good steward of your body, soul, and spirit. We've got to do right with our bodies. Even though my appearance didn't have that "dashing" appeal, I began to feel better about myself. I often wanted to lay in the bed and pity my present situation, but my mother would make me get up, in order to maintain a level of activity. I even began to do small chores again around the house. These small activities showed me that life goes on, and you've got to get up and fight for your life.

The days, weeks, and months began to pass by as my mother, an ordained Reverend and Evangelist to Jamaica, planned for me to go with her to the island of Jamaica. I was ecstatic about the trip, because I was going back to the place where I formally lived when I was younger. My mother and I thoroughly enjoyed our time on the tropical island. We went to the beach, ate great food, and my level of energy began to regenerate. The epic moment of that trip was going to church in Jamaica, where our good friend, Pastor Paul Johnson invited my mother and I to join him. My mother played piano and sang during the service.

I was notified some time ago that the Pastor wanted me to speak at his church. So, he introduced me and gave me the microphone to speak. I was so nervous, I thought about how people might perceive my appearance and baldhead, but I gathered myself, stood straight, and told the people that I had been diagnosed with Cancer, but despite the report from the doctor's I believed that I was healed, in the name of Jesus. As I spoke, many people were crying and clapping, but I began to use scriptures that were put into my heart at a young age. I said, "I won't believe the doctor's report, but I will believe the report of the Lord." I let them know that I will fight the disease and will defeat the enemy in order to declare the works of the Lord. I stood and spoke with boldness, because the Bible says, "The righteous are as bold as a lion (Proverbs 28:1)."

As I look back on the day when I was speaking, I know it wasn't me, but it was God speaking through me. When I finished speaking, the Pastor and congregation prayed that the power of God's healing would manifest in my life. From that moment on, a fire was birthed within my bosom. The fire of Faith, the fire of Determination, the fire of Perseverance, the fire to fight for my life, burned within my spirit. This fire quickened my spirit, to say, "Yes, I will overcome Cancer." The prophet Jeremiah said, "It's like fire shut up in my bones (Jeremiah 20:9)." My spirit was elevated and my mind was reinvigorated, in spite of my current situation.

The Bible declares, "Now faith is the substance of things hoped for the evidence of things not seen (Hebrews 11:1)." I might not see the victory in my current situation, but I believe that my victory is on the way because, "I walk by faith and not by sight (II Corinthians 5:7)." When your situation looks bleak, and people tell you, "It's not going to happen," that's the time for you to switch on the gear of faith and hold onto the Word of God. If you hold onto doubt the outcome will be doubtful, but if you hold onto the promises of God through His Word, your end will be victorious.

I began to believe that I was healed, in spite of the way I appeared or felt. The way I left the United States was not the same way I returned in my trip from Jamaica. I returned with a new outlook on life, my countenance was different, and people saw a change in my demeanor. I wasn't the "Old sluggish Eddie," I didn't pity myself, or cry, "Woe is me." II Corinthians 5:17 declares, "If any man be in Christ, he is a new creature, old things are passed away; behold all things have become new." The Greek transliteration for the word *new* is *kainos*, which means unused, fresh and novel. When you give your life to Jesus Christ and serve Him, He begins to invigorate your spirit, refresh your mind, and resurrect your life.

I began to thank God for each day that I was blessed to see. As I continued to receive even more chemotherapy, I didn't enjoy it but I bit my lip and endured it, knowing that I was one step closer to total restoration. I began to count my blessings because other individuals, past and present have died from Cancer, but I'm still alive by the grace of God.

You ought to know that it's only by the grace of God that you are still here. Other people who were more intelligent, better looking, wealthier, or even more talented than you are gone, but you're still standing. The accident didn't kill you, the overdose didn't wipe you out, the abuse didn't destroy you, and the mental anguish didn't obliterate you, because it was God who covered you in the storm and when the waves were about to take you under, He swooped in and grabbed you out.

Oh, you're not alive because of your good looks, you're not alive because of the degrees on your wall, you're not alive because of your grandiose eloquence, charm, or socio-economic status, but you're alive because God has a purpose for your life that He wants you to fulfill. You will never be fulfilled, until you have completed what God has ordained for your life.

There are people in this world with riches beyond measure, living an affluent and glamorous lifestyle, but they aren't fulfilled. The fact of the matter proves that happiness is not in what you possess, but in who is possessing you. If the cares of this world possess your life you will live an unhappy life, striving but never thriving inwardly. You can possess everything, but never progress in anything. That is why we must let the Spirit of God possess the very nature of our being, because without Him there is no sustained happiness. I can hear Solomon, the wealthiest yet wisest man who ever lived, crying out, "All is vanity and vexation of spirit (Ecclesiastes 1:14)." A man who has accumulated everything, realizes he has nothing. As he looks over his life at the decisions made, he discovers that his pursuit of pleasure has ended in pain.

We must not allow the substratum of our living to be in vain, but every minute that we spend on this earth should glorify God and help somebody as we travel along. As I began to gain inner strength, my physical strength began to increase. There were days after receiving treatment that I would feel sick, but the feeling would subside and I'd be right back up on my feet again, moving in the direction towards total healing. My physical condition began to increase, because my spiritual connection to God invigorated my situation. Your condition should never determine your connection to God, but your connection to God should always impact the state of your condition. You've got to be so connected to God that even if you're battling financial instability, you'll still praise Him or if you're sick you'll still worship Him. The scope of your praise shouldn't be predicated on your position, but the magnitude of His power, which will ultimately redirect your position in a positive manner.

Even though you might have received a bad report from the doctor, your money looks funny, or your life is dark and full of despair, you've got to know that, "Weeping may endure for a night, but joy is coming in the morning (Psalm 30:5)." I don't know how long you've been weeping, maybe you've been weeping internally for days, months, or even years. Yet, if you're still weeping, know that God isn't through with you.

I can personally say that in the midst of my battle with Cancer, God dried my tears and the sun began to shine again in my life. The sun will shine again in your life. Your situation is only temporary, because Jesus is a deliverer; He is a restorer, and what seems to be a temporary set back will become a permanent stepping-stone. For, "Greater is He (Jesus) that is within you, than he (the devil) that is in the world(I John 4:4)." If we know who resides inside of us, we can defy that which is outside of us. Your inner character can overcome the outer calamity of this world, your joy can override sadness, your peace can maneuver through perplexity, your love can defy the hater, and your faith can overcome fear. I believe if we really knew the depth of who we are and what we're made of, we would overcome every situation by the power of God. You're too extraordinarily intelligent to allow ignorance to run your life, you're too beautiful to be battered and abused psychologically, physically, and emotionally. Its your time to get in the fight, but not by your flesh, for the weapons of our warfare are not carnal (II Corinthians 10:4). This is a spiritual fight, because you can fight on your knees in prayer. Fight for your life, take control of your mind, take control of your space, and take control of your life. For, "Whom the Son hath set free, is free indeed (John 8:36)." I had to fight to be free, because there were many days I wanted to throw in the towel, but I had to muster up enough faith, determination, motivation, and inner volition to overcome the odds. While I was fighting, I knew I wasn't alone, for this battle wasn't mine, it was the Lord's (I Samuel 17:47). In the resurgence of my strength, I could tell that God was doing a work in my body. I was still receiving chemotherapy and radiation treatments, but my level of strength after the treatment increased from previous times. The doctors would run tests and chest x-rays but couldn't find a trace of Cancer.

With every test and x-ray, my faith increased, the enemy would try to bring thoughts of fear upon me before the tests, but I told the devil, "You are a liar, I'm healed by the stripes of Jesus, and I shall live and not die." The Bible declares, the devil is the father of lies, because he is the author of the lie and he can't do anything else but deceive you, (John 8:44). You've got to rebuke the devil and tell Satan the blood of Jesus is against you. That's the only way you'll have the victory.

Your intellectual prowess can only take you so far, your gift of gab can help you every now and then, your stunning beauty and debonair style might get you off the hook sometimes, but its something about the name of Jesus that supercedes all things to deliver and save you from the uttermost to the gutter most. It's His power that prevails beyond all obstacles and opinions. It's because of God's power that you're still here. You should have been killed in the car accident, you should have overdosed, you should have tested positive for AIDS, you should have been in an insane asylum, you should have been killed, and I should have died of cancer, but God. Those two words, "but God" have saved our lives. I should have, I could have, and I would have but God has restored, resurrected, reinvigorated, reenergized, and renewed us so enormously that we've got to reintroduce ourselves to those who have counted us out and thought we'd never make it. The detractors thought I would never make it.

Purposefully Prepared to Persevere 17

I remember seeing a former acquaintance, some years ago, and he was aware of my dealings with Cancer. We fell out of touch for a certain amount of years, but on one occasion I ran into him and said, "Hey man, how are you doing?" At first he looked puzzled, trying to figure out who I was, being so flabbergasted in awe he replied, "I thought you were dead, we all thought you died of Cancer." I immediately felt a disappointing rush flow through my body, but I responded emphatically, "I'm not dead, but I'm alive and well," as he could see. I've realized folks are so fickle that when you fall, they think you're down for the count. Yet, when your situation looks bleak, when it looks absolutely dead, that's when God rushes in and resurrects us by His power. He reaffirms your vision and anointing, so now you can look at the "haters" and say, "You thought I was dead, you thought I was gone, but I'm back, I'm back with more power, I'm back with more joy, I'm back with a vengeance to destroy the enemy, because I've been resurrected and redeemed by the mighty hand of God." Oh I hope you can feel the power of passion and determination being exercised through these words. There is a power that prevails beyond our circumstances and that power is the Lord Jesus Christ. Let His power invigorate your life, engross your love, and enlarge your territory. His power had to be evidenced in my life, because He has healed my body and raised me up to thwart and repel the onslaughts of the enemy, in order to compel you through courage. As I went through Cancer my value seemed to depreciate, because in the prime of my teenage years, through my experiences, I wasn't able to be a teen like the others. I wanted to feel accepted among my peers. I wanted to hang with the crowd, but I felt ostracized because of my experience with Cancer. The "friends" that should have been there were (MIA) Missing in Action. We don't need so-called friends in our lives, but we need friends that can get in the fight with us, especially when the wall of despair and destruction becomes so high that we can't seem to get over it. I don't know about you, but I need individuals in my life that can propel me beyond the hurdles of life, and pour the power of purpose into my soul.

The absence of my father in my life, especially during my battle with Cancer has impacted my life beyond measure. My father was in the home, but then again he wasn't in the home for some years of my life. He was there but he wasn't there, if you can understand. To a certain degree, it's ambiguous as well as contradictory, because he was given the role as father, yet he did not perform in the given role as father. So, through my parents' divorce, my mother was the strong catalyst of my formative and adolescent years of life, operating in the role as mother and father. Oftentimes, my brother and I joke with my mother on Father's Day and say, "Happy Father's Day Mom." Oh yes, we buy her cards, balloons, and shower her with the whole gamut of gifts, because she has successfully performed in the dual role as both mother and father. She even taught me how to kick a football, which still amuses me to this day. I can empathize with the young man or woman who didn't grow up with a father in their home, because I wasn't born with a "silver spoon" in my mouth, but I had to work hard to be successful. So, growing up was tough for me, because my father never poured into me. My dreams at a tender age were to play in the NBA, and my father played basketball on the collegiate level. I just wanted him to take me under his wings and train me to achieve my ultimate dream. I was so perplexed, because he just wouldn't do what needed to be done. I found myself studying basketball tapes hours on end, practicing to perfect my skills, when he could have helped in the process of expanding my talent. I wanted him to help me achieve a level of greatness, but I began to tread that road alone. I wanted him to help me achieve a level of greatness, but I began to tread that road alone.

So, since my father wasn't there and didn't supply my needs or the needs of his estranged family, I began to look to other men for guidance. I adopted successful men as "father figures," such as athletes and movie stars. These types of people, were individuals that I couldn't touch or dialogue with, yet symbolized an idealistic concept of excellence. For instance, when I was growing up, Michael Jordan was the man that I wanted to emulate. I wanted to "Be Like Mike," just like the catchy advertisement suggested. On screen, he was everything my father wasn't. Yet, the isolation and estrangement from my father gripped the very core of my heart. As young people, we internalize loss in so many different ways. That's why mother and father in the home as parents are such an integral component of the growth and maturation process of young people. Our young people internalize loss in various ways by joining gangs, promiscuous behavior, suicide, drugs, alcohol, abuse, and so many other ways, because we're looking to be validated. The problem is that the streets and the world are giving more value to our young people than parents, schools, churches, etc.

The world's value consists of devaluating an individual, in order to fit the schema of society. That's why the Bible declares, "Train up a child in the way they should go, and when they are old they will not depart from it (Proverbs 28:6)." Many of our children and young people are lacking training, so the world is quick to grab them up and turn them out. America's youth are crying out for internal healing. Our youth have experienced everything on the outside, but are vexed with hurt on the inside. The abuse experienced at a young age has left scars on men and women. The traumatic experience of the breakdown of a family has left individuals brokenhearted, and so many other causes have stemmed from the discombobulated state of a nation. Yet, in spite of the circumstances, I serve a God that is able to turn trials into testimonies, turn prostitutes into preachers, turn junkies into judges, and take you and me and set us free. The prescription for the maladies in America are not found on Wall Street or in the hierarchical chains of government, but are found in the Word of God, "For if my people, which are called by my name, shall humble themselves, and pray, and seek my face, and turn from their wicked ways; then I will hear from heaven, and will forgive their sins, and will heal their land(Chronicles 7:14)."

The Bible affirms that when father and mother forsake us, then the Lord will receive us, (Psalms 27:10). I don't have to be strung out on drugs because one of my parents abandoned me. There's no need to go looking for love and validation in all the wrong places, because I can look to the hills from whence cometh my help, for my help comes from the Lord, (Psalms 121:1). Yes, I can say daddy wasn't there, but don't let "there" stop you from getting to "where" you want to go. Don't sing the sad song, or the "woe is me" line. You might have to cry, but go on and cry, because weeping may endure for a night but joy is coming in the morning, (Psalm 30:5). Your father or mother might have left you, but Jesus said, "I'll never leave you nor forsake you," (John 14:18, Hebrews 13:5,6). People come and people go, but Christ is always there. So, lift up your head, be encouraged, God is the strength of your life. I'm an example that Jesus will heal the hurt, He'll wipe the tears, He'll restore the years, and He'll calm the fears. Just like the old song says, "I came to Jesus just as I was wounded, weary, and sad but I found in Him a resting place and He has made me glad." I want you to be glad. Yes, people and situations might have made you weary, wounded, and sad, but you must forgive, loose it, and let it go because in Christ is joy unspeakable and life more abundantly. Despite your negative experiences there is a positive outcome, looming on the tail end of your victory. There is strength not only in forgiving others, but also in forgiving yourself. To totally move forward, you've got to let something go, because it will continue to weigh you down and ultimately crush your spirit. Never let your problems crush you, instead crush your problems. You are here to be a beacon of light to those in dark places and invigorate others with your strength and testimony. However, you can't do that if you're still holding onto the problems and mistakes of yesteryear. If there's one thing that you do, "Forget those things which are behind and reach toward what is ahead. Press towards the goal to win the prize for which God has called you heavenward in Christ Jesus (Philippians 3:13,14)." You can't run forward while looking back. As we often do that, we bump right into another problem, continuing in a cyclical way of life, with no forward progression. If you're ever in pursuit of something, it's going to take power, passion, and persistence to overcome any hurdle, in order to propel yourself to the desired goal. There will be obstacles that arise, but each and every obstacle tests your character, tests your determination, tests your desire, tests your inner volition and evaluates the scope of who you really are on the inside. Sometimes it takes falling to get up and even sometimes it takes failing to succeed.

Life is not lived on one-plane or steady stream. Life is like the heart monitor in the hospital, it's up and down, changing, and it often fluctuates. Yet, if the "heart monitor of life" flattens, your life is extinguished, you become numb, and you need to be revived. The people in our world need to be revived. Our world has become numb to the needs of the people that inhabit it. The hearts of men and women have grown cold, towards one another, to the point that we can't empathize or sympathize with each other's pain. The search for peace has drawn individuals to addictions of all kinds, whether it's sexual, drug related, etc. Yet, the industries and marketing affiliates are playing and profiting on addictions and maladies, as it's preying on the lives of our people. We're becoming extinct and desensitizing our cognitive abilities and moral senses. The power of marketability and capitalization are vanquishing our young peoples minds to the point that they have now become a commodity or pitch sale. Our world has moved beyond the scope of community and has now incorporated almost every facet of life as a commodity. For instance, more value is placed on a human body's outward appearance than a human beings inner character. There are more television shows and commercials on self-aggrandizement and outward adorning, than shows that speak to the power of esteeming value and self-worth in the lives of individuals. We've become numb to offensive behavior and "shock television." Most can say, "I've seen it all," and "It doesn't surprise me," because the rudiments and the age of this world have become entrenched in Godless behavior, which has corrupted the minds of individuals. Now is the time, for people to come together on one accord and stand up for righteousness in our neighborhoods, stand for excellence in our school districts, stand for ethical behavior in our business sectors, stand for conviction in our judicial systems, stand for Jesus in the face of judgment, stand for freedom in spite of inequality, and stand for love in the face of haters. Let's face it people, we've fallen for lies, tricks, schemes, and anything else we can imagine. Now is the time, to stand for something that's awe inspiring and positive, not just for us, but also for the common good of all mankind. There's no need to be afraid for Ephesians 6:10 implores us, "Be strong in the Lord and in the power of His might. Put on the full armor of God so that <u>you</u> can take your stand against the devil's schemes." The thirteenth verse states, "Therefore put on the whole armor of God, so that when the day of evil comes, you may be able to stand your ground." There's no need in going out to battle unarmed. There's no need in standing for your convictions without a solid foundation. The armor and Word of God is a sure foundation, for the evil days are here and people of strength are needed to go out and reclaim lives in our land. You can't stand against the devil's schemes without power or the anointing of the Holy Ghost. In today's times, you've got to be armed for battle and dressed with power. Its one thing to be dressed debonair or sophisticated outwardly, but your spirit must have an inward dwelling and tailoring by the power of God. To be able to overcome Cancer, to reclaim what the enemy stole, or to live a victorious life you've got to wear the belt of truth, the breast plate of righteousness, you've got to wear shoes of peace, the shield of faith which will block the fiery darts of the enemy, you must wear the helmet of salvation, and possess the sword of the spirit, which is the Word of God. Yet, after being armed and dangerous, you've got to continue in prayer and watch with all perseverance, (Eph. 6:14-17). You are a soldier of strength, a man of might, a lady of liberty, a freedom fighter, and a child of God. So, you can tell the enemy I shall not fear, I shall not capitulate because, "Greater is He that is in me, than he that is in the world (I John 4:4)." Please tell the haters, "Nay, in all these things I am more than a conqueror (Romans 8:37).

If your detractors seem forgetful just remind them, "I can do all things through Christ that strengthens me (Philippians 4:13)." Yes, I know you might feel like you're all alone and you cry sometimes but remember, "Weeping may endure for a night but joy is coming in the morning (Psalm 30:5)." You might get tired, but God will renew your strength like the eagles, you'll run and you won't get weary, you'll walk and you won't faint, (Isaiah 40:31). So, don't get tired in doing well, because you'll reap a harvest of blessings if you don't faint, (Galatians 6:9). You possess the endurance within your spirit, so just keep on fighting.

Chapter Two

"2" EXTRAORDINARY "2" BE ORDINARY

I truly believe that the inner trials and outward circumstances that an individual endures and overcomes, distinguishes him/her from the masses. I Peter 2:9 states, "You are a chosen generation, a royal priesthood, a holy nation, a people belonging to God, that you may declare the praises of Him who called you out of darkness into His marvelous light." It totally befuddles me at times, that despite what we go through, or even put ourselves through which often devalues our perception of ourselves; God has still chosen and called us to be his royal workmanship. Jeremiah 1:5 declares, "Before I formed you in the womb I knew you, before you were born I set you apart; I appointed you as a prophet to the nations." God has esteemed, established, and orchestrated your life, in order for you to be a blessing in someone else's life. God created humanity in His image and everything that He creates is designed to fulfill a specific purpose. In this world, we're looking to validate who we are. Many of us are on a quest for self-knowledge. Yet, we often search for validity from the wrong things. Your value isn't tied to the clothes you wear, the man or woman on your arm, the newest vehicle on the street, or the accoutrements that we accumulate. Your value is nestled in the gifts and talents that God has placed deep in your bosom. The Bible declares, "We have a treasure in earthen vessels, that the excellence of the power may be of God and not of us (II Corinthians 4:7)." In order for you to understand yourself, you must begin to understand your creator. God is the manufacturer of our lives and we are the product of his creation. Since we were created and designed by God, we ought to emulate our creator. We ought to think Godly, behave Godly, and speak Godly because God is our source of power. If your spiritual cord is plugged into the outlet of His Word, God will illuminate your life. Yet, our world is in a chaotic state and humanity has malfunctioned from the state of the way the manufacturer (God) designed. God doesn't operate by rocket science, but by simple principles. You don't have to understand Maslow's hierarchical structure to understand God, and you don't have to understand Newton's theory of relativity to know that God loves you. Yet, people often associate God with a false sense of mysticism. However, understanding God is not mystical, all it takes is your faith. The Bible states, "For if you have faith as a grain of mustard seed you will say to this mountain, move from here to there, and it will move, and nothing will be impossible for you (Matthew 17:20)." God loved you so much, that he sent Jesus, His only begotten son to earth, in order to die for your sins (John 3:16). Yet, as we expand the parameters of our thoughts concerning ourselves, we must understand that God is pristine, magnificent, splendiferous, omnipresent, inexplicably creative, and undoubtedly powerful. Now, with all of that magnanimity innate within His character, this is the same God who has infused Himself into your spirit. The Bible states, "God created man in His image (Genesis 1:27)." The aforementioned passage means that God infused His characteristics, His person, His intellect, and His creative abilities into humanity. God has placed within the deep inner-recesses of your soul, a timeless treasure that exceeds years, backgrounds, ethnicities, or ages. You are blessed with a distinctly different gift that distinguishes you from the masses. You are distinct and distinguished. God didn't ordain your life according to the cyclical age of time, but according to the constructs of eternity. Romans 8:29 states, "Whom He did foreknow, He also did predestinate to be conformed to the image of His son Jesus." God foreknew you, meaning He knew you before He ever created the world. There are two Greek interpretations for the word "know," which is about the foreknowledge of God. The first being *yada* which means to perceive, to distinguish, to recognize, and to be acquainted. The second interpretation deals with the word *ginosko* which means prognosis, *ginosko* is the knowledge that has an inception, a progress, and an attainment. So, God *yada-ginoskoed* you, meaning He knew you before He ever predestinated your life. God has pre-destined, pre-determined, pre-evaluated, pre-arranged, pre-announced, pre-approved, pre-conceived, pre-conditioned, pre-judged, pre-meditated, and pre-viewed your end before your beginning. The scriptwriters and directors of movies, like Steven Spielberg and Spike Lee, do this for a living. They film the ending of the movie first and then retrofit certain scenarios in the beginning and middle portions of the movie, in order to bring about the completion of the story. This sounds like something God does, except He's been doing this before time even began. God determined your outcome before time began. You think what you're going through is a stumbling block, but it's only a stepping-stone. The fiery trials of life participate in the cultivation of your character, which ultimately brings you forth as pure gold, (I Peter 1:7). There is an inward power that will transform your outward circumstance, there is a bubbling brook of joy that will overshadow the mudslides of mayhem, and there is a radiant expression of sunshine that will peer out of the dark clouds in your life. The source of this great inner wealth is Christ Jesus. For He is the one that can mend the broken hearts, deliver the captives, and bring sight to those that are blind, (Luke 4:18). In this day and time, there is an irrevocable call that speaks to the hearts of young people. There is a call to the masses, yet individual in nature, that tugs at the hearts of young men in the ghettos of America, there is a call that reverberates in the caves of calamity to conquer the circumstances that have conquered you, there is a profound purpose for the young woman, who is struggling to maintain her self-esteem in spite of debilitating experiences. There is a call that compels young people to reach for righteousness, rather than fall prey to the trappings of this world. There is a symphonic sound of solitude and stability that seeks to provide a balm to the wounds of abuse, negative childhood development, and enslavement of the mind. Young people no longer can we live as our own worst enemies, in a prison without bars. The time is now for deliverance from self-destructive behaviors, the time is now to step out from among the crowd and cultivate your vision, now is the time to esteem value into your schools and communities. To my inner city brothers and sisters, you must use the talents and innate God-given gifts, to mobilize others and yourselves beyond the shackles that seek to keep you bound. The African-American people have been blessed in the arts, athletics, and various musical genres and are world-renowned, but we've also been blessed with knowledge and wisdom in our minds. To the young

Purposefully Prepared to Persevere

man and young woman, you have the wherewithal to exceed in every aspect of academia, but you must apply yourself to reap the benefits of your labor. "Study to show yourself approved unto God a worker that does not need to be ashamed, rightly dividing the word of truth (2 Timothy 2:15)." To move from where you are to where you want to be takes vision, power, and your ability. As young people we've been called the Hip-Hop Generation, we've been called the X-Generation (because they can't figure us out), we've been called the MTV Generation, and its often argued that this generation knows more, understands more, is technologically minded, has seen breakthroughs in health and science and has even been on the bitter end of tragedy with September 11th, the AIDS epidemic, drug use, the demise of the family, promiscuity, and teenage pregnancy. Our generation has been ostracized, scandalized, endured trials, and tribulations. But young people I want you to understand the importance of being connected to God, understanding His love for you, and being renewed in the spirit of God. You are too extraordinary to be ordinary and its just not enough to be apart of the Hip-Hop Generation, the X-Generation, or the MTV Generation. The passage in I Peter 2:9 claims, "You are called to be apart of the Chosen Generation, you're called to be a royal priesthood, a holy nation, a peculiar and extraordinary people that will lift up the name of Jesus Christ." Your value in Christ, esteems your value in life. Your value isn't predicated on how many diamonds are in your chain, or how gaudy your earrings are, because nothing in this world is congruent to the price of your life. You are totally unique and not a duplicate. Your fingerprint is different from six billion other individuals on the face of the planet, YOU, yes YOU are fearfully and wonderfully made (Psalm139:14). The world is in search of Christian young people that are going to be real. They're searching for radical, no holds barred young people that will stand for righteousness and declare that Jesus is Lord. The world is searching for that real young man and woman. The spirited cry of America is declaring, "I'm searching for you in your school, I'm searching for you in the mall, I'm searching for you on the basketball court, I'm searching for you on the college campus, I'm searching for you on the cheerleading team. Where are you? Stop hiding and stand up for what you believe in." People are hurting and searching for the remedy to the ailments of life. There are people in this world who are hurting and searching, lonely and searching, partying all night but searching, sleeping around and searching, yet asking, "Where have all the young Christians gone?" Everybody has mixed in with everyone else and no one can discern between good and evil. Yet, I propose that you and I might be the only Bible that someone ever reads. Someone may never read the Bible, because they're reading our conduct. They're listening to what we say and observing how we treat people. Yet, the substratum of this resounding call is that God is calling us to deeper commitment. The focus of youth in America has been displaced and misplaced. Our lives have been misdirected and put out of focus, due to the maladies that we've endured or placed upon ourselves. We've embraced style over substance, fashion over drive and passion, promiscuity over purity, and popularity over personality. Our television programs and musical hits have begun to determine the methods by which we think. We've begun to internalize the messages that others are streaming into our minds. Our self-concept has been radically altered, because of a style that is popular to emulate or an ideal persona that a man or woman is pressured to possess. Meanwhile, the world has got us frantic and our lives are in a conundrum, because as the world turns we turn. Stop right there, and gather your thoughts. Be yourself and cultivate the ingenuity and intelligence on the inside of you. The gifts and talents that reside within you are just an expression of the timeless treasure that you are. You have been handcrafted by God, to be the best that He created you to be. You don't need a smooth rapper to tell you how fine you are, you don't need a sleek and sophisticated vehicle to esteem your value, you don't need astounding apparel to give you a new attitude. Yet, you must allow God to fix you up, mold you, make you, shape you, and take you up to where He's called you to be. Let God give you an internal makeover and allow Him to be your inward tailor. There is an inward beautification and renewing that God provides through His Word. David the passionate psalmist cried, "Create in me a clean heart O God and renew a right spirit within me (Psalm 51:10)." If you're looking for the tangible fountain of youth to maintain your vigor, ebullience, or debonair style, you won't find it. The overflowing source of inner power and vitality is in Jesus Christ. There is an inner void that only Christ can fill and when He fills it, you'll be able to say like the song declares, "This joy that I have the world didn't give it to me and the world can't take it away." Through the tests and trials of life, I had to learn that satisfaction doesn't come in the reactions and attractions of this world, but in a relationship with Jesus. God didn't heal and raise me up from Cancer to live a mediocre life. He restored me, so that I could restore those that are lost. He gave me a testimony, to share how He brought me through the tests of life. He gave me power, to overpower that which sought to destroy me and crush the devil's head in the process. We can all say that we've had our back against the wall, whether at one time or multiple times and whether you acknowledge it or not, God made a way of escape for you. There are people who have capitulated and died to what you've been delivered from. So many people are diagnosed with all types of diseases, yet God healed you. You could have been destroyed in the car accident, yet you survived. You could have been paralyzed from a hit you endured on the football field, yet you're walking. The doctor told you that you couldn't have children, yet you've raised two of them. Your bills were due on the 30th, yet someone gave you a check on the 29th. There's no need to live oblivious to your blessings, you know you're blessed. You've survived what people have succumbed to, you've defeated what people were defeated by, and you have been blessed with the strength to remain positive despite negative circumstances. Ecclesiastes 12:1 implores us, "Remember now your creator in the days of your youth, before the difficult days come, and the years draw near." You've got to establish your relationship with God while you are young, before the evils of life harden your heart. God isn't waiting for you to serve Him when you're old and finished doing what you've desired to do. He wants you to serve Him now, with all the energy, vitality, and ability you possess and the creativity that is nestled in your mind. God has called us in Romans 12:1 to "Keep our bodies as a living sacrifice, holy and acceptable unto God, which is our reasonable service." It is our duty to keep our bodies holy unto God. We must avoid sinful acts of the flesh and self-destructive tendencies or behaviors that harm our bodies, because our bodies are the temples of the Holy Ghost. But why, you may ask? The passage in I Corinthians 6:20 states, "You are bought with a price: therefore glorify God in your body, and your spirit which are God's." The previous (19th) verse reminds us that we are not our own, because the body in which we reside doesn't belong to us, but it belongs to God.

As God sent his son Jesus to die for you, He paid the cost of your indebted sins with His shed blood on Calvary. For instance, you attend prom or an elaborate banquet with your date, so you rent a tuxedo or an elegant gown. You read the bylaws and sign your name, guaranteeing you'll bring the attire back in one piece. So, you purchase your attire and walk out of the store. You and your date attend the event together, but you want to be careful with the attire that you're wearing, so you don't slide all over the floor and start doing the splits, because you know if you bring the tuxedo or gown back to the store ripped, tattered, or torn there will be a price to pay. You instead act accordingly that night in a civilized manner and return the rented apparel to the store, the way it was given to you, because even though you wore it, it's not solely yours, because you're only renting it. God is declaring, the body I gave you isn't yours, but it belongs to me because you're renting it to do the job that I've designed for you to accomplish. So when you present yourself to me I want you to be a living sacrifice, holy, and acceptable. I want you to be pure in your words and your deeds. You have been charged and commissioned by God to raise the roof of righteousness, because you're destined to destroy the devil. God has given you His Word, now just walk in it. For His "Word is a lamp unto your feet and a light unto your path (Psalm 119:105)." As you give your total self to God, He gives His total self to you. That's why He wants you to praise and worship Him, because your power is in your praise. In John 12:32, the writer makes a significant declaration that there is drawing power in the name of Jesus. For Jesus said, "If I be lifted up I'll draw all men unto me." The power of Christ will draw you out of the hurt, He will draw you out of the pain, He will draw you out of sin, He will draw you out of guilt, He will draw you out of self-destructive behaviors, He will draw you out of fornication and promiscuity, He will draw you out of addiction, He will draw you out of poverty, He will draw you out of abuse and misuse, He will draw you away from the haters grasp. Christ will draw you out of low self-esteem, and whatever you're dealing with, cast your cares on Jesus, for He cares for you, (I Peter 5:7). So come to Him, because He will draw you out of every circumstance, just activate His power, assume the position, access His presence, and He'll annihilate the opposition on every side.

In Matthew 5:14 the passage declares, "You are the light of the world." You are a beacon of light in dark places. The world is waiting in expectation, for the revelatory evidence of the light that Christ has placed inside of you. You ought to enlighten the world with your gifts and talents, light up the world with your power, light up the world with your wisdom, light up the world with your joy, light up the world with your song, light up the world with your ministry, light up the world with your testimony, light up the world with the effulgence of your intellectual prowess, light up your school with power, light up your neighborhood with esteeming value, wherever you go illuminate the place. In order to bring light, you must be illuminated by God and He declares for you to "Come out from among them and be ye separate says the Lord (II Corinthians 6:17)." God is calling you and He's compelling you to come out from among the masses. Now is your time to emerge from the crowd and be the leader in your community, shake yourself from the shackles of self-pity, rise up out of the ashes and infuse power into someone's life. Young man it's your time to isolate yourself from the gang of peer-pressure and "so-called friends" that secretly seek to destroy you. Young lady now is the time to set your priorities in order and redeem

Purposefully Prepared to Persevere 35

your value in life. Show the light from within, stop hiding, and show who you really are. Pick up the phone of life, God is calling you. The same way Jesus raised up Lazarus, He's raising you up. Lazarus come forth!! You might be bound up, but God has decreed you to be loosed and let go. God has loosed you from the grave of grief, He's reclaimed you from the depths of despair, and He's orchestrated your final outcome. You might be hurting but come forth, disappointed but come forth, broken in spirit but come forth, abused but come forth in the name of Jesus. Don't hide your gifts any longer, don't hide your dreams, don't hide your vision, don't hide your intelligence, don't hide your ingenuity, but throw your shoulders back, walk with your head high, and be who God has called you to be. The Psalmist declared, "Lift up your heads O ye Gates and the King of Glory shall come in (Psalm 24:7)." This is your time to emerge from the crowd and stand for Jesus, come out from the masses and declare that Jesus is Lord of your life, show yourself, break out of your shell and be who God destined for you to be. God has given you the power, to defeat the enemy in your mind and destroy him on every side. You are a King's kid, you are a chosen generation, and you are royalty in Christ. God designed you as His light source, to illuminate the world with the treasures He's placed inside of you. The Apostle Paul declared in Ephesians 2:1, "You hath He (Jesus) quickened who were dead in trespasses and sins." The word "dead" means *nekros* in the Greek and denotes separation or demise. Yet, God has made you alive, despite your former state of living in the carnality of this world. This is not a physical death, but this is a spiritual death, because you were spiritually separated from God and connected to the sensations of the world. Before God came into your life, you were walking by your flesh, you were comatose, you were trifling, tripping, and wayward. You were "A sinner formerly known as" and I'm sure you can fill in the space. Oh yes, you were so dead that you didn't even have a spiritual pulse. Yet, God picked you up and took you into the operating room of ICU, His Intensive Care Unit, and placed the Automatic Electronic Diffibulator of His Word on your life and said, "I've come that you might have life and have it more abundantly (John 10:10)." So, God reinvigorated your spirit, He revitalized your mission, He renewed your mind, He reinvigorated your vision, He revived your passion, He reaffirmed your anointing, and He's restored what the devil stole. So, now you know and you're fully assured, "If anyone be in Christ, he is a new creation, old things are passed away, behold all things have become new (II Corinthians 5:17)." You've got to know who you are and whose you are. If you know whose you are, you'll shake off doubt, fear, and unbelief because Jesus will "Keep you in perfect peace, if you keep your mind stayed on Him (Isaiah 26:3)." For, "God has not given us a spirit of fear; but of power, and of love, and of a sound mind, (2 Timothy 1:7)." If you know whose you are you won't allow individuals or circumstances to debilitate your confidence because, "You can do all things through Christ that strengthens you (Philippians 4:13)." If you know without a shadow of a doubt that God is your source you'll understand, "No weapon formed against you shall prosper, and every tongue that rises against you will be condemned (Isaiah 54:17)."

Chapter Three

POWER PERFECTED THROUGH PAIN

An individual once declared, "Strength is not measured in the good times, but in the bad times." For us as the people of God, we can surely affirm that hard trials will come, storms will blow, situations will arise, peer pressure will rear its ugly head, and every trick of the enemy will try to divert our attention, from the victory that God has ordained for our lives. Yet, through it all, there is an intense charge to blockade the enemy's attempt to break your spirit. Oh, I know it can be rough and tough at times. I know we feel like giving up at times, but we can't allow any devil or individual to manipulate or destroy the gifts that God has placed inside of us. There is a central concept that arises and encourages us to be stronger, because of the trials that we have overcome. You've learned to smile in the midst of sadness, and take it in order to make it. When you've done all you can, the Spirit of God will impregnate His power within you to endure adversity, therefore Perfecting His Power in you to endure the Pains of life and come forth victoriously. Through the struggle, through the pain, through the heartache, and through the shame you must press your way to victory. We may be hard pressed on every side, yet we don't have to be distressed, or depressed, (II Corinthians 4:8-10). So, despite the obstacles, there's no need of stressing because God has already provided the blessing.

Every one of us has faced some type of adversity in our lives, and if you haven't faced it yet, just keep on living. You will learn that life is not always a bed of roses, and you will often find that there are thorns attached to those roses. Oh yes, many of us have learned to be more cautious, because everything is not as it seems. I've often found myself in the desert stage of life and a mirage of water would flash before my eyes. Yes, it was ebullient and profound, but as I pursued to delve in, nothing was there and my plan eluded my grasp. Through the various stages of our lives, the ups and downs, twists and turns, the seemingly ebullient roller coaster rides of life have often brought us to a screeching halt, wondering how can we find some stability in our lives. Yet, the fact that we're still here lies in the undeniable concept, which is immersed in God's providential preservation of our lives. Each time we're in a predicament, the enemy tries to twist our hands and drown us in the depths of our problems, <u>but God</u> delivers and brings us to the top of the surface because of His purpose and plan for our lives, (Jeremiah 29:11). Your Power is greater than your Pain. Your inward Character is greater than your outward Circumstance. As individuals, we tend to look at the <u>obstacle</u> rather than the <u>outcome.</u> Many of us are traversing through the course of life and we know we've been called, chosen, and gifted by God to do exploits. So, as we're on the course of life, walking the straight and narrow path, opposition may arise, depression may knock at our door, temptation my sneak out of the bushes, financial instability may be prevalent, and even the "haters" may come out of the woodworks. So, immediately the enemy will seek to attack your mind, because he poses as a, "Roaring lion, seeking whom he may devour, but you must resist him steadfast in the faith (I Peter 5:8,9)." For if you, "Resist the devil he will flee (James 4:7)." The enemy seeks to attack your mind with fear, doubt, dismay, and thoughts contrary to the Word of God because his strategy is to, "Steal, kill, and destroy," but Christ came to endow you with life more abundantly, (John 10:10). I've often wondered why *kill* precedes *destroy,* it seems as if the two words should be reversed. However, the words are synonymous, because if the enemy kills your drive or will to live, your life is already destroyed. While the word *kill* refers to "putting an end to by means of death," the word *destroy* refers to "breaking in pieces." So, not only does the devil want to put an end to your life, but he wants to demolish, break, and scatter your life. The devil wants to annihilate you in anyway he can. The enemy desires to weave and deceive you spiritually, so that you're always chasing and never grabbing, looking for fulfillment yet never satisfied. The enemy wants your relationship so polarized from God, that you assist him in destroying yourself. The devil wants you to help him commit assisted suicide on your behalf. The devil hates you because you are made in the likeness of God and when he looks at you, he sees you in the image of God's creation. So, if the devil can choke your joy then he's happy, but when God renews your joy he's furious. Never partner with the enemy, because you make his job easy. All the devil wants you to do is live a life that is offset from God, by never accepting the work of Christ on the cross for salvation. Yet, through the matriculation of salvation, many of us never abound to the vastness and splendor of the purpose of Christ in our lives. So, the negative self-concept of ourselves overshadows the power of God, because we don't step out of our comfort zone. If the enemy can keep you comfortable, he can manipulate your mind into conformity. Yet, Romans 12:2 declares, "Be not conformed to this world (godless age) but be transformed by the renewing of your mind. Then you will be able to test and approve what God's will affirms, His good and perfect will." The enemy wants to debilitate you psychologically, so that you engage in destructive behaviors, and live your life in a revolving manner, with no forward progression. However, on the flip side, what the enemy seeks to debilitate in your life, God is ready to rehabilitate, because those schemes that the enemy devised to destroy you, God will flip the script and restore you, in the likeness of His glory. Don't lose your mind in the situation, don't capitulate in the midst of the battle, and don't misplace your cognitive space in a seemingly horrible matter. You must change your mind for victory, you must eject negative thoughts, infuse thoughts of positive outcomes, and you must see excellence as the only option because you can only change your mind by the anointing and power of God. The mind is the key to unlock the doors to your visions and dreams. Yet, if your thoughts are contrary to the Word of God, negativity will reside and the receptors of your mind will control your tongue as you speak, which will then transform into the constraints of your actions. That's why the Bible implores us, "As a man thinketh in his heart so is he (Proverbs 23:7)." Your thoughts are the platform, upon which you stand, and your thoughts ultimately govern your life. The mind is a central unit that stores information and it is the means by which short-term and long-term memory abides. The mind is photo-oriented, so anytime that your thoughts are conceptualized, pictures or images are formed in your thought process. For instance, if I said the word "dog" to you and told you that I walked the

Purposefully Prepared to Persevere 41

dog around the block, you would automatically see an image of a dog in your mind, whatever color it may be is to your discretion. My point is the mind doesn't think words, your mind thinks pictures and images. So, whatever we allow into our minds, especially through the conduits of our eyes and ear gates, is what we will process and the information we attain will infiltrate itself into our spirits. So, if you meditate on negative propaganda or sensually oriented material, these concepts will rewind, fast forward, and play in your mind and you will find yourself meditating on falsehood principles rather than truth-ridden promises. In order for you to move out of the meandering, discard the mediocrity, and elevate from where you are to where you need to be, you've got to renew your mind. There's no need in moving to a new environment with an old mentality. The environment doesn't necessarily change the individual, but the individual changes the environment. So, in order for you to to change your situation, you must allow God reconstruct your mind. You can remain positive in a negative situation. Not only will God change your situation, but He'll also change you in the situation and release you to change that which sought to debilitate you. God has authorized you to be a change-agent, and He'll bless you with a double testimony, so that when you witness to someone, you won't just tell them what God did for you, but you'll also tell them what God did through you. He restored your life and now you experience abundant peace, He strengthened your character and now you exhibit self-control, He blessed you financially and now you're sowing back into the ministry. Sometimes we've got to press our way, in order to move the stress out of our way. I'm reminded of the woman with the issue of blood, (Matthew 9:20). The Bible declares, "She said within herself, if I could just but touch the hem of His garment, I shall be made whole." Sometimes to reach the level of healing or a desired state of totality, you've got to encourage yourself. You've got to encourage and motivate yourself through through the predicaments of life, and talk to your issues. On the bed of Cancer, I had to motivate myself through the Word of God, in order to break down the walls of my circumstances and breakthrough to healing and deliverance in my body. To overcome obstacles in life, it takes inner volition and an intense fire inside that makes you roll up your sleeves, ball up your fists, and grit your teeth. You've got to be so tenacious in defying the enemy and the haters that be, that you'll say to yourself, "I might go in limping, but I'm coming out leaping." You might be crying in the circumstance, but when it's over you'll be smiling. If you want to achieve that dream, you've got to be focused and determined because the enemy will design detours to destruction. You've got to tell yourself, "I will overcome, I will breakthrough, I can't stay like this, but I must get up." You must arise and arrive to the level of destiny, because you're Destined to Overcome the Odds. So, get up and take back your life, keep pressing, keep moving, and keep going. David said, "I will encourage myself in the Lord (I Samuel 30:6)." All your friends might have "tipped" out on you, everyone else may be doing their own thing, but you must be determined to make it, even if you have to make it all by yourself. When everyone else scatters, God is still there to calm your fears and dry your tears because, "He'll never leave you nor forsake you," (Hebrews 13:5) and when the enemy thinks you're at the end of your rope and seeks to "Rush in like a flood, the Spirit of the Lord will lift up a standard against him (Isaiah 59:19)." You are going to make it in spite of the pain, because its stirring up your power, the pain is working towards your prosperity, and the times of sadness are invigorating gladness. So, don't fret, because, "All things work together for the good to them that love God and are called according to his purpose (Romans 8:28)." Your circumstances will bring about a positive end, because you are called to greatness and you have a great purpose in the earth. You've been through too much to give up now, because you have Power that's being Perfected through Pain. Right through here, the word "Power" has four transliterations in the Greek. The first being *dunamis* which means might, or great force. The second is *exousia* which means the authority or right to act, its your ability, privilege, and delegated authority. The third usage for "Power" is *kratos*, which denotes dominion, strength, and manifested power. The word signifies exerted strength, and this is power shown effectively in a reigning authority. Now the fourth usage is *energes* and this is energetic power, this denotes power that is at work, active, and effective. We must understand that God has given us an immeasurable amount of power. He has given us dominion, His Word, and His Wisdom but many times we sit on our gifts and the power He has given us, by falling prey to the traps of the enemy. The power of being perfected in Christ is not through your collaboration with the enemy, but in your resistance to the devil's schemes. The Apostle Paul esteems us through exhortation, "Count it all joy when you fall into various trials, knowing that the testing of your faith produces patience (James 1:2, 3)." Our joy is perfected through what we endure. So, because of our mistakes, the trials and temptations, the downfalls and frustrations, and the negative treatment we've endured, it instills within us the power to forgive, the power to love, even the power to say, "God bless you," in the face of an enemy and really mean it. The power that God has endowed within your spirit, the *duna-*

mis, exousia, kratos, and *energes* are continually being perfected. The Bible invigorates our spirits and reminds us, "Our strength is made perfect in weakness (II Corinthians 12:9)." The pressures of the world are releasing the power, that's within your spirit. The weak times and moments, in your life, are being cultivated and molded into strength, in order for you to control that which the enemy controlled prior to your deliverance. So, the word "perfected" means to complete, accomplish, carry through to the end, reach a goal, and fulfill. The word "perfected" denotes maturity. In I Corinthians 13:11, Paul speaks about his development and writes, "When I was a child I spoke as a child, I understood as a child, I thought as a child: but when I became a man, I put away childish things." In order for us to develop spiritually, we must endure the growing pains. It's no use for us to enhance our physical structure, to the point that we're robust and well nourished on the outside, yet remain anorexic and suffer from spiritual malnourishment on the inside. There must be a balance in our lives, so that we progress outwardly as well as inwardly. The Apostle John declared, "Beloved, I wish above all things that you would prosper and be in good health even as your soul prospers (3 John 1:2)." There must be a dual development in your life, where positive growth and forward progress can occur. Through the maturation of your character, there must be a determining factor that moves you from Pain to Power. No one can move forward, while holding onto the past, "If a man put his hand to the plow and look back, he is not fit for the kingdom of God (Luke 9:62)." Your life is powerless, if you continue to rehearse the painful circumstances you've endured. The circumstances will ultimately choke and shackle the freedom that God has made available to you, unless you take hold of His power. The Apostle Paul declared, "Forgetting what is behind and reaching toward that which is before me, press toward the mark (Philippians 3:13)." You've got to reclaim your life, because God has given you a new lease on life. You're not designed to carry stress, burdens, pains, and internal weariness but, "Cast your cares on Jesus for he cares for you (I Peter 5:7)." Take your burdens to the Lord and don't take them back with you, but leave them there. The Bible declares, "Do not be anxious about anything, but in everything by prayer and petition, with thanksgiving, present your requests to God (Philippians 4:6)." Why are we dealing with the stress and allowing our blood pressure to rise, biting our nails, being frantic, and behaving in a discombobulated manner? Stop and just relax. Christ is our burden-bearer, so unload all your baggage and give your problems to the problem-solver. There's no need to self-medicate our pains. There's no need to hold onto our pain, with a woe is me attitude. There's no need to harbor bitterness towards others, because if you don't release the pain you'll destroy yourself and others from the inside out. You are not a destroyer of lives, but you are a restorer of lives. The negative conception of life, must be replaced with the positive reception of living an abundant life. So, your past must be replaced by your future. If your past consisted of hate, your future must consist of love. If you're harboring bitterness, you must cultivate forgiveness, and if your beginning was negative, your ending must be positive. You've got to understand, that when you hand the keys of your life over to God, He will open doors that no man can shut, He will open financial doors, He will give you favor wherever you go, and He will, "Prepare a table for you in the presence of your enemies (Psalm 23:5)." God will prepare what you need in the presence of the "haters," yes, even in the presence of the so called "movers and shakers."

God will wipe away your tears, He'll calm your fears, and He'll redeem your years, (Joel 2:25). For God is the "Balm in Gilead (Jeremiah 8:22)." The Lord is your physician, for He will provide the antiseptic of His Word to the wounds and maladies of your life, in order to bring about healing in your life. The doctor might have given you a prescription, but God has provided the remedy. The power that was released by Jesus, on Calvary's cross, has been made available to you. You don't have to live a painful life, because you are called to live a powerful life. You might have gone in ravaged, but you're coming out rejuvenated. God is birthing a greater power in your life, so that your praise will crush the enemy's head. Since your Power has been Perfected through Pain, it now becomes a Platform of Praise to God. Not only is your power perfected, but your praise is perfected and directed in the path of purpose. For, "Out of the mouths of babes and infants, God has perfected praise (Psalm 8:2, Matthew 21:16)." God will allow you to go through the pages of your life, in order for you to arrive to at the new chapter of your life. So, now when you look in retrospect, as to where God brought you from and where He's taking you, you'll have a new shout, and you'll have a new praise. When you dance for joy, it won't be out of emotion, but sincere devotion. Your thankfulness to God, won't be a rendition of tradition, but it will be immersed in perfect praise. You were created to praise and worship God, so everything that can inhale and exhale has a reason to praise the Lord (Psalm 150:6). There is Power in Praise, Purification in Praise, and Provision in Praise. So, Praise is a Purifier of Pain through the Power that God endows upon your behalf. The problems that were magnified become microscopic when you begin to praise, worship, and magnify God. The praise that you offer up to God, extracts and releases

Purposefully Prepared to Persevere 47

you from the junk of sin, by inviting the Spirit of God to rest, rule, abide, and set up residence in your spirit. The book of Psalm is an ode to praise. David, the gifted and talented psalmist, composed many mellifluent and melodious songs of poetry. In Psalm 34:1, it was David who wrote, "I will bless the Lord at all times and His praises shall continually be in my mouth." Yet, it was this same individual, just a few chapters later in Psalm 42:5, who was burdened in his heart and began to ask himself a series of questions, "Why are you cast down, O my soul, why are you so disturbed within me?" Yet David esteems himself, by responding emphatically, "Put your hope in God, for I will yet praise him." The aforementioned passage is proof, that you can be on cloud nine one day and stuck in the mud of despair the next day. However, how you respond when your back is against the wall, that will determine how high you rise or how hard you fall. So, David gives us a glimpse in these verses, of an ebullient care-free praise and then a down-trodden circumstance, which must be transformed into positive self-esteem and uplifting praise directed towards God. There's no need to allow situations to get the best of you, because you've got what it takes to overcome, for, "The Lord is a shield for you; He's the glory, and lifter of your head (Psalm 3:3)." David didn't give place to negativity, and he didn't allow the enemy to toy with his mind. We can no longer be puppets in life, we must be puppeteers, if we desire to be in control of our lives. I ask you, who's pulling the strings in your life? If people, traps, temptations, addictions, and schemes of the enemy are pulling your strings, then you aren't in control. Yet, if God is directing your life than you are free, "For who the Son (Jesus) has set free is free indeed (John 8:36)." I'm no longer bound by sin, but I've found in Him a resting place and He has made me glad.

Praise is the conduit, by which God bestows His blessings on you, for when the praises go up, God's blessings shower down on your soul. Praise is not just a word or method to happiness, but it's a lifestyle. It's so extraordinarily profound, because if you were to delete the letter *P* from the word *Praise* it would read, *raise,* and that's what you do every time you open up your mouth, to give the Lord thanksgiving and celebration. Each time that we *praise* God, we *raise* Him higher, and as we *raise* Him, He *raises* us. Every time you erase doubt and fear from your mind and focus on determination and faith in Christ, you raise the Lord above your problems. So as Christ rises, I rise. As I lift Him up, He lifts me up. As I lift Him up above my circumstances, He lifts me up above my circumstances. James 4:10 declares, "Humble yourselves in the sight of the Lord, and He will lift you up." If we concede our plans, our egos, and our desires to God, He will strengthen us. In Psalm 121:1, 2, the scripture declares, "I will lift up my eyes to the hills, from whence comes my help? My help comes from the Lord." We should lift our eyes, our hearts, and our hands to God, because He is our provider and our strength.

Chapter Four

YOU ARE GOD'S MASTERPIECE

For us as individuals, living in a world that is predicated on what we have, rather than the strength of who are, can diminish our value in the way we perceive ourselves. The defining factor comes down to the fact, am I looking at how the world views me through its eyes, or am I looking at how God views me through His eyes? Our perception and conception of our value in life is important, because we often have a proclivity to become sidetracked, when we begin to accumulate possessions. For instance, you once were living in a one-room house, now you're living in a six bedroom palatial estate. You didn't have an attractive vehicle, but now you've got a monstrous SUV that when you come to a stop, the rims keep on rolling. Oh yes, before you were sad, bad, and mad, but now you've got one of those "Bling-Bling" smiles that when you show your teeth, you look like a Colgate toothpaste model. On the outside, you're a debonair man or a gorgeous woman, but on the inside you're still miserable. You can be blessed on the outside, yet busted and disgusted on the inside. However, God wants to fuse your personality and your prosperity together, so no area of your life is lacking, but every area of your life is abounding in the magnitude of God's power. An individual's quantity does not determine an individual's quality, because you can have absolutely nothing and still be a person of substance. The power to live is not contained in what you have, but it's contained in who you are. You can live a life where the world changes you, but you never change the world. You can traverse through life and live to the extent, where everything on the outside is different, but everything on the inside remains the same. Whether you've got ten, one-hundred dollar bills or ten, one dollar bills in your pocket, you've still got to know who you are. The richness of life isn't one-sided, as to where it's only contained in the vastness of one's financial stature. Yet the riches of life are contained in discovering one's purpose of living. Your purpose _for_ living and your purpose _of_ living are two separate entities. An individual could have a purpose _for_ living, which is tied to accumulating possessions or personal fulfillment. Yet, in that supposed purpose _for_ living, one's true purpose _of_ living could simply be to enhance the scope of their world and the lives that he or she encounters. The power of living is enhanced, when an individual can extend their hands to someone who is trapped in the cave of calamity, or headed towards a detour to destruction, and rescue them, in order to impart value and substance into their lives. I heard an individual declare, "If I can help somebody as I travel along, then my living shall not be in vain." Our impact in life is not only direct, but also indirect. The decisions that we make today, will affect future generations tomorrow. The life we live on a daily basis is constantly affecting our surrounding areas, families, and acquaintances. We must not capitalize on, and exploit, the lives of others, but we must energize and instill value into the minds of others, in order to be critical thinkers and change the systems that have brought about spiritual, social, and economic demise. In Matthew 16:26 Jesus declared, "For what profit is it to a man if he gains the whole world, and loses his own soul?"

The Apostle Paul composed a beautiful treatise of the Gospel, which gives validity to our daily lives in Christ. In Ephesians 2:10 Paul states, "For we are His workmanship, created in Christ Jesus for good works, which God prepared beforehand that we should walk in them." We are God's workmanship and the Greek transliteration is *poeima*, which means to make. The word signifies the universe as God's creation and the redeemed believer as His new creation. You are God's masterpiece, because you were created to accomplish good works. You weren't created to be defeated, you were created to live a victorious life. By understanding who we are and our relationship in Christ, it brings us to the highest heights and the deepest depths of self-knowledge. For God is the manufacturer and you are His masterpiece, which He has created you to be the gift that enhances the lives of others. God has given you His ultimate gift, by sending Jesus to die for your sins and redeem your life, in order to lift you from the doldrums of death and catapult you to the apex of atonement. In the second chapter of Ephesians, the Apostle Paul wrote and conveyed a profound message, in order to bring us to complete cognizance of the fact that our own works or deeds did not bring us to salvation, but the redemptive work of Christ on the cross has brought about our spiritual freedom. Christ became the ultimate sacrificial lamb and scapegoat for our sins. You and I couldn't have paid enough, to prevent Christ from being whipped, bruised, beaten, and hung on a cross. Christ's love and passion for us, propelled Him to the cross of Calvary. The same love that He exemplified for you and I, allowed

Him to endure the crown of thorns, which was vigorously forced into the parietal, occipital, and temporal lobes of His skull. He was nailed between the radius and the carpal bones of His wrists, which cut the media nerve. Christ was nailed between the inter-metatarsal space of His feet, that sent a blaze of inextinguishable fire and trauma through His body. Oh yes, Christ endured the excruciating and cataclysmic extirpation physically, but He sought to redeem the sins of mankind spiritually. Each beating that Christ endured released our healing. Every nail that was driven through His skin, released our power. Isaiah 53:5, "But He was wounded for our transgressions, He was bruised for our iniquities: the chastisement of our peace was upon Him; and with His stripes we are healed." Christ became the ultimate sacrifice and died for us, so that we could live for Him. Christ paid the bill for all of the sins we committed and made it a love payment. We were bound to sin and indebted to captivity. Yet, the same God that canceled our debts, is the same God that reorganized, reevaluated, reestablished, renewed, regenerated, and redeemed our lives. The accomplishment of Christ at Calvary, institutes value in the lives of every human being that will accept it. So, since Christ has forgiven us, then why can't we forgive ourselves? I understand that we've been hurt in our lives and we've also hurt others, but God did not bring us to condemnation, because He became the propitiation for our sins. Romans 8:1, "There is therefore now no condemnation to them which are in Christ Jesus, who walk not after the flesh, but after the spirit." Christ provided reconciliation and if we are going to be new creatures in Christ, we've got to be reconciled to God, but we also must be reconciled to ourselves. I can't disassociate me from myself, because I have to live with me. After the party is over, after the friends have left, and after you've laughed as hard as you can, you still have to deal with yourself. The people who have walked in and out of the doors of our lives are gone, but some of us are still hurting because the stain of the memory resides within our souls. Even though the person is gone they are still present, because we haven't relinquished the pain. So, the emotional bruise has now festered into a self-inflicted wound, because it's still present in our minds. Every time we wallow and waylay in the past, we cut ourselves, and slowly commit emotional suicide, because we haven't relinquished the scars and bruises of yesteryear. The cycle of self-destructive tendencies and behaviors is personal, because we begin to hurt ourselves and we hurt others, due to the former pain we experienced at the hands of other individuals. In the process of hurt and pain, we hold onto the stain of the memory, but when we release and relinquish the pain, we release ourselves from the pain. Your internal conflict constrains your upward mobility, it holds your feelings captive, it stifles your expression, and it lowers your expectation level, to where you don't anticipate the best because its been lowered by others. All of a sudden, here comes God and He says, "Come unto me all ye that labor and are heavy laden and I will give you rest (Matthew 11:28)." We've got to let God work on our inward parts, the inner parts that no one else can see. David cried, "Examine me, O Lord, and prove me; try my mind and my heart (Psalm 26:2)." Sometimes we've just got to fall in the arms of God. A man's arms can't take care of your problem, a woman's arms can't take care of your circumstances, but the arms of God will provide all that you need and soothe the pains of life. You are God's prized possession and the epitome of His creation. We are God's masterpiece, but there are still things within us that need to be mastered. We've put up a façade too long. Sometimes we come to church dressed in our masks, as if it were a masquerade ball, looking clean and sharp on the outside, but discombobulated and dirty on the inside. Oh yes, the image is impeccable. The men are debonair on the outside and the ladies' hair is whipped, dipped, fried, dyed, and laid to the side, but the enemy has been whipping us on the inside. Some of us have our Gucci and Louis Vuitton accounts, but our lives aren't necessarily accountable to the Word of God. Yet, in my life I've learned that it's not what's covering me, but it's whose covering me that matters. If we let God cover us, He will give us whatever we need, because He will cover it. You are God's workmanship and you are His masterpiece. Everything you've been through, solidifies and stamps you approved by God. You had to go through the orientation of His Word, so that you could become a new creation by His Word. I John 4:19 states, "We love Him because He first loved us." I serve a God who possesses so much love, that He can hate an individual's sin, yet love an individual's soul. I serve a God that can take a liar and make them a lawyer. I serve a God that can take a prostitute and make them a preacher. I serve a God that can take a drunkard and make them a deacon. I serve a God that can take a junkie and make them a judge. I serve a God that can take you and me and make us free indeed. I know you've got to be God's masterpiece, after all the tests and trials you've endured and you're still standing. I know God has done and is continually doing a masterful work in your life. Before I met Christ, my life had no rhyme or reason, but now that I'm in Christ, He's brought symmetry, balance, and order into my life. You are God's poem. You are God's work of art. You are God's melodic symphony. You are God's grandiose display of excellence. You are God's handiwork. You are the expression of God's creativity. You are the love of His life. You are His heart's desire. You are His model of magnitude. You are His expression of elegance. You've got what it takes to be great, because God has placed greatness inside of you. Don't you dare, let anyone debilitate your self-esteem and don't let circumstances or your living situation devaluate your character. Whenever someone says, "You can't," respond with, "I can do all things through Christ that strengthens me Philippians 4:13)." If your dream has never been reached before, you go out and reach the apex of your dream. So what if it's never been done before, you go out and accomplish it. You must centralize your focus and rid yourself of distractions, that will thwart the progression of your future. You are a masterpiece and not a mess, because you were created in the image of the splendiferous and magnanimous God. We must look into the mirror of the Word of God and if our reflection doesn't reflect God's image, then we must allow Him to make us over. If the Word of God is reflecting faith, but our lives are a reflection of fear, then we must allow God to alter our spiritual image and self-concept. Money, material possessions, and people don't provide total happiness and aren't the answers to our problems. You are the answer to your problems. The accoutrements of this world and the people that inhabit the world, won't provide consistent happiness and joy, because peace and serenity dwell within us. So, as long as you try to change yourself by yourself, you will continue to be unhappy. Yet, when you let God change you from the inside out, all things will become new. The answers to your problems, are nestled in the treasure within your spirit and the dispensation of God's salvation. Now, you must dig deep within your soul, by discovering the gold mine of freedom and purpose that's nestled inside of you. If God designed you to be His masterpiece, why are you living in mediocrity? No longer must you reside in the ways of old, but God is calling you to abide in His power. In Psalm 91:1, the scripture declares, "He that dwells in the secret place of the Most High shall abide under the shadow of the Almighty." God wants you to reside in His everlasting love. Sometimes the walls of our life crumble, in order to focus our attention on the true essence of our existence. The situation had to break you down and bring you to your knees, so that God could build up your faith. Yes, even the relationship had to breakdown, so that God could break you into His Word. Our own theories, prognostications, and solutions are not enough to solidify our stance in life. You can have a solution to a problem, but no resolution. You can know what's wrong with something and yet not know how to solve the problem. I can tell you that God not only knows how to solve the problem, but He knows how to resolve the problem and bring closure. When we try to fix our own problems, they're still open-ended. Yet, when God fixes our situations, He finds a way to deal with our problems and the substratum of who we are, by closing the case and sealing the deal. Oftentimes, the problems in our lives are like sentences ending in commas. Yes, that seems strange, because by our own merit we can't provide complete closure to the problems of life, but only God can replace the commas in our lives with a period and pronounce it, "End of story."

Chapter Five

I WON'T GIVE UP

In Galatians 6:9 the scripture declares, "Be not weary in well doing, for in due season we shall reap if we faint not." In the deep recesses of the substratum of our humanity, there is a proclivity to give up when the deluges of life seem too much to bear. When the ravages of disease come calling for your mortal soul, when tragedy seems to overcome all of your triumphs, or when heartbreaks become heartaches, how will you approach the situation? Will you approach the negative by Fear or by Faith? Will you capitulate or will you put on your combat armor? Will you speak what the Lord says, or will you speak that which everyone else is telling you to say? We must make decisions that will direct our lives in a positive manner, no matter how infinitesimally small they are or how grandiose they seem to be. Our correct and positive decision-making comes from God, who is the maker of all creation and the author of our salvation.

Psalm 46:1 states, "God is our refuge and strength, a very present help in trouble." The trials and troubles of life seek to debilitate us but the strength of God is here, even now, to rehabilitate us in the midst of trials and troubles. God is not only going to fix your life after you've come through the storm, but even in the midst of tempestuous trials and tribulations, God is fortifying your faith, He's cultivating your character, and He's solidifying stability in order to radically reshape your resilience. Now, is the time for God's work to be done in your life, which will then begin to manifest in the lives of others. You have been etched in God's Hall of Faith, as an overcomer. You've come too far to give up now, you've crossed too many hurdles to "Let the chips fall where they may." Yes, you have come too far to let your life break into pieces. The doctor may have given you a negative diagnosis, but God's got the final prognosis. You've pressed against the wall of worry long enough, but release your hands, and you'll notice the muscular definition that you've now acquired. You've got too much life to live for to allow death and negative trials to take you out. You've got songs to sing, dreams to fulfill, ministries to be birthed, families to bless, testimonies to tell, you are a chosen vessel of God. You ought to proclaim to the enemy and every debilitating situation that comes your way, "I shall not die, but live, and declare the works of the Lord (Psalm 118:17)." Your life is not meaningless, but God has preserved you for a purpose. You must shake off distractions and doubts and live in victory, live in excellence, live in power, and declare that healing is yours, declare that power is yours, declare that peace is yours, declare that you won't be defeated but you will be uplifted in the name of Jesus. You've got to declare that you are an overcomer by opening your mouth and speaking it, "For death and life is in the power of the tongue (Proverbs 18:21)." Now after you've declared that which is in accordance to the Word of God, launch out and live in victory. God is looking for individuals who possess a "Never say die attitude" and who refuse to give up. For those individuals who have survived cataclysmic circumstances, greater power is infused, in order to strengthen the lives of others. It is incumbent upon us to not only exhibit the outward display of strength, but to exhibit the strength that is within us. For the whole notion of the matter, is that either it's in you, or you're without it. We must possess the strength of God, that will hurdle us over the tough times, temptations, and frustrations that life often presents. You must have the strength of God, on the inside of you that can muster up some joy in times of sorrow. You need the strength of God to combat the fiery darts of the enemy. You need the strength of God to tell the "haters," "God Bless You," when your flesh wants to curse them out. You need the strength of God, so that you won't get weak when your trial looks bleak, but you'll activate the power button of peace and you'll, "Walk by faith and not by sight (II Corinthians 5:7)." Right through here, we've got to understand that giving up is not an option, because "The trying of our faith produces patience (James 1:3)." Our inner-will must be locked into God's Word, so that we can remain joyous in the midst of pain, exhibit power to persevere, and approach heartache with happiness. Despite the madness, the notion of truth is exhibited, to the fact that we can't allow our circumstances and situations to depreciate the value in our spirits, because when our flesh gets weak, God will renew our strength and deliver us with His mighty hand. The Bible declares, "For though our outward man perish, yet the inward man is renewed day by day (II Corinthians 4:16)." God is steadily fortifying and purifying our spirits through His Word. So, every situation that presents itself as a stumbling block, God will transform it into a stepping-stone. Don't fall prey to the traps, pressures, or supposed setbacks of the enemy. As we endure various situations that come to defeat our minds, bodies, and spirits, God has granted us the Favor, to have the Fervor, in order to endure the Fire. The Bible compels our hearts and gives the title of "light affliction," to the various situations, circumstances, trials, hardships, and tribulations that we endure in life. Yet, at the heart of the matter, our light afflictions are only for a short time and work for us a "Far more exceeding and eternal weight of glory (II Corinthians 4:17)." I stand today as a Cancer survivor, and in retrospect of the pain I endured, I viewed it as hardship and literally as hell on earth. Yet, at the same time, it was the best and worst event of my life. I was confronted with the Word of God, I was confronted with the enemy's plan to wipe me out, and I was confronted with the state of myself. Yet, when the enemy sought to bring about my demise, God flipped the script and used it to display His work of healing. I didn't view Cancer as "light affliction" during the process, yet after God healed my life, I can attest to the power that is continually being regenerated in my spirit. I can see the development of my spiritual muscles of perseverance, so that what is inside of me becomes greater than my outward circumstance. The Bible declares, "Greater is He that is in me than he that is in the world," (I John 4:4). I refused to give up on my life and there were many days that I wanted to quit. There were times when I felt like giving up. I felt the pains of loneliness, anxiety, dismay, and perplexing pressures, but I made it through the rough times, and if I can make it, I know that you can make it, too. God is upholding us with His right hand and He's no respecter of persons. He will deliver you, just like He delivered me.

Yet, on the other side, sometimes we can be our own worst enemies. We can oftentimes live in the revolving door of trials and circumstances that we bring on ourselves. Rather than going forward in life, we take the circular path. Rather than extinguishing the fires that have burned our lives, we continually fan the flames that have kept us bound. Oftentimes, we don't put the blame on ourselves, but we place it on others and lash out at the individuals in our lives that really love us. We play the blame game and say, "If it wasn't this way I would be here or there." However, the "should've, could've, and would've" stories of life, will only detract our momentum in reaching our goals. You had dreams and aspirations many years ago, that never came to total fruition because you let a roadblock offset your vision. Yes, I know you might not have been raised in the most grandiose household, Daddy might not have been there, you might have been abused, you may have been teased in school, and you might have even lived on the streets. However, there is a resounding call, that places the responsibility on us. Situations and people might have hurt you, but how will you handle it? Will you live a life of pity or will you overcome with power? We can't continue to blame our fathers, we can't blame our family members, mothers, sisters, or brothers. We can't continue to blame the white man or the black man, the community, or past events. Your life might have been scattered, but God will endow you with the strength to pick up the pieces of your life. Yes, I know the situation sought to destroy you, but God is here to restore you and esteem your value. Don't look for people to change, but become the change that you want to see. Be who your father never was, accomplish what he never accomplished, and become what he never became. Be the beacon of light in dark places and the strong tower for those who are weak. I can attest to the fact, that in life, the road to recovery can be an arduous process. Yet, we must no longer take detours to destruction and paths that lead to spiritual poverty, but forge ahead to the futures of freedom.

You are a survivor, you are a fighter, you are person of prominence and you must continue to conquer that which seeks to conquer you. For, "Nay in all these things we are more than conquerors (Romans 8:37)." I went from Cancer to Conqueror, to More than a Conqueror. Yet, between the interval stages, I discovered that the Character of a Conqueror is cultivated in the chaotic, catastrophic, cataclysmic, and calamitous circumstances of the life cycle. You've got to gather the creativity, gifts, talents, and energies of your mind and submit them under the power of God, in order to endure the fires that seek to bring you to ashes. If you want to come out more powerful than you came in, you've got to have a strong and courageous mind, because God is with you, (Joshua 1:9). Yes, storms may come, winds may blow, tides may rise, but if your feet are planted on the rock named Christ Jesus, you will win. It is here then, that God is calling for fighters, that can be likened unto a Fire Fighter, in order to quench the flames of the enemy, (Ephesians 6:16). God has given us the water hose of his Word, in order to extinguish the fires that the enemy, has set ablaze in our lives. You've got power to extinguish the fires of fear and you've got power to subdue the fires, that seek to destroy you. God is searching for those who will look at trouble, as an opportunity to triumph, fear as a chance to exhibit faith, and financial instability as an opportunity to ultimately prosper. Can you look at your situation and defy the enemy? You've been hit, but you're not down, you've been bruised, but don't give up the fight. You can't give up and you can't take any detours. I learned that you can't go over it, you can't go under it, you can't go around it, but you've got to go through it, because the outcome of the blessing is too enormous to take a shortcut. I've discovered that it's either all or nothing at all. The world is waiting for your testimony; don't capitulate in times of hardship because you'll reap a harvest of blessings if you don't faint, (Galatians 6:9). In a troubling and confused world, you've got to stand on the Word of God, for Christ is your anchor. He is the author and the finisher of your faith, (Hebrews 12:2). You're too close to capitulate, go back and revisit your dreams, revisit your visions, write it and make it plain (Habakkuk 1:9, 10), don't neglect the gift that is within you but stir it up (II Timothy 1:6), and bring forth the power that is nestled within your spirit. We need the power and love that God has placed inside of you, to launch out and captivate the hearts and minds of young people. We need your volition and energy to revitalize our communities. Our nation and world is waiting for you to bring value back into our educational institutions and school systems. The scope of our worldwide forums and governments need those who can revive the constructs of righteousness, honesty, financial insight, and ethical behavior into our very forms of life. Our churches are depending on you to lead, when others have passed on. We need you to be the change agent in a world that is yet searching for hope. God has authorized you to be the wellspring of life, that refreshes the atmosphere with the aroma of your anointing, the splendor of your song, the pageantry of your poetry, the compelling character of your charisma, and the words that flow from your wisdom. The greatest gift that you could ever give to the world is not your possessions, but the product of your purpose, which permeates the very hearts and minds of those that you encounter because God has destined you for such a time as this, (Esther 4:14).

Chapter Six

MY MIND IS ON A MISSION

Peter Forsythe declared, "Unless there is within us that which is above us, we shall soon yield to that which is about us." There must be power ingrained in our hearts that flows from God, which will propel us beyond the paralysis of peril. God has commissioned you, to complete a specific mission in this world. You are equipped with the proper talents, gifts, and inner-drive to forge you along the path of success. You weren't born in a specific geographical location, time, month, day, or year for no apparent reason. Yet, God has strategically pre-arranged your life in this time to impact generations. God has given you the supply of His Word, in order for you to apply it in your daily life, for He has given us this day our daily bread (Matthew 6:11). We must steadily feed our spirits with the nutrients of God's Word, thereby we can defeat the spiritual onslaughts of the enemy on every side. If we take a glimpse into the Word of God and analyze the various men and women contained, we will understand that God's work is always accomplished through human beings. The scope of God's work is often completed through human intervention, where mortal man is the conduit of the power of God that enhances the lives of others. In order for God's mission to be birthed and completed in our lives, we must not only grasp it spiritually, but also we must grasp it in our minds. God wants to occupy, inhabit, and take up residence in your mind. The radiant beauty of God's Word that ultimately redirects our lives and passions, comes when we begin to internalize His word in our spirits and minds. You were brought to this planet for a specific purpose in mind. You have a special task to complete, and the only way for you to receive revelation of your delegation, is to seek the God of your salvation. God is the only one that can breathe into your spirit and awaken your mind, to appropriate the hope of His calling that He has placed in your life. In order to navigate through the conundrums of chaos and the caves of calamity, you've got to understand that you have been planted on planet earth to fulfill the mission that God has designed for your life. Isaiah 26:3 reminds us that God will keep us in perfect peace, if we keep our mind on Him. The enormity of your mission on earth will push you beyond the pains of life and keep you afloat, beyond the tides and winds that seek to take you under. God has granted you with "Peace that surpasses all understanding which will keep your hearts and minds through Christ Jesus (Philippians 4:7)." Understand that anytime God gives you a mission, it will require faith, spiritual fortitude, and an unwavering mind. The ability to complete your mission in life, will depend on the strength of your mind, because only the strong will survive. In the scope of our commission from God and the completion of our mission in life, there will be sacrifices, hurdles, and trials between the commission and the mission stage. Once you come to the full cognizance and are absorbed in the anointing of God, the enemy will seek to oppose your stance like never before. It is incumbent upon us in the times between our authorization (commission) and application (mission) that we remain steadfast, unmovable, and always abounds in the work of the Lord, (I Corinthians 15:58). As we traverse in expectation of the excellence of God's glory, we may not see quick results of our mission, but we must never allow the opposition to debilitate our disposition. Upon Jesus' ascent into heaven, after He rose from the dead, He spoke emphatically to His disciples and said, "Go ye into the entire world, and preach the gospel to every creature (Mark 16:15)." The commission was to "Go" and the mission was to "Preach to the world." Yet between the commission and the mission to the disciples, the word "Ye" (you), is a central element of Christ's departing words. The only person that can fulfill the call, that is nestled in your heart is you. The only person that can stop your mission from coming to fruition is you. Yes, people may pose as distractions and situations may come to detract your mind, but you are the one responsible for crossing over the hurdles and temptations of life. No matter what people say or what comes your way, when it looks as if the Mission is Impossible you've got to tell yourself in spite of the opposition, the Mission is Possible. For, "With God all things are possible to them that believe (Matthew 19:26)." Power is possible in times of weakness, love is possible in times of hatred, and overcoming is possible in times of opposition. You must remain vigilant, believe in God, and march through the storm with your mind focused on your mission. Right through here, the Apostle Peter challenges us to prepare our minds for action by remaining sober, self-controlled, and setting our hope fully on the grace to be given at Christ's revelation, (I Peter 1:13). God wants us to not only look at where we have been, where we are, but begin to look at where we can be. Many of us reflect on the

Purposefully Prepared to Persevere 67

hurts, disappointments, and trials of yesterday, but God is trying to focus our mind on the blessings of today. If you can focus your mind and your mission on your vision, then the vestiges of your past will be only a blur, because your future will be as bright as the noonday sun. The mission of your mind is to grasp the call of God, and not only to grasp it, but also to apply it in your daily life. God has called you to complete the mission that He's designed for you, because "The gifts and the calling of God are irrevocable (Romans 11:29)." You are gifted to guard, you're gifted to guide, you're gifted to galvanize, and enhance the lives of others. You've got to press towards the mark for the prize of the high calling of Christ, (Philippians 4:14). What goal(s) are you eager to reach in life? Don't run after the goal and run past God, but run towards Christ and He will propel you to the goal(s) that you're striving to reach. Keep your mind on the Lord, keep your mind on the goal(s), keep your mind on the mission set before you, and wherever your feet shall trod, step on every opposition. Now, is not the time to be debilitated by circumstances, but be the catalyst that is energized by the Word of God and conquer the enemy. God has not given you a spirit of fear but of power, and of love, and of a sound mind (I Timothy 1:7). The word "sound mind" denotes discipline, good judgment, and self-control. James Allen once declared, "Only the wise man, only the one whose thoughts are controlled and purified, makes the winds and the storms of the soul obey him." It is what you can't see in me, that will transform the circumstances of my life that reside outside of me. The beauty of who you are isn't predicated on the physical magnitude of your outward appearance, but is contrived in the deep thoughts and innerpower that lies within your spirit. King Solomon, who was known for his insightful wisdom declared, "For as a man thinks in his heart so is he (Proverbs 23:7)." This scripture gives credence to the fact that an individual is literally what he or she thinks, and their character is nestled in the scope of their thoughts. The seeds that are planted into the soil of our minds, will eventually take root and spring forth good or evil in our lives. If we don't guard our minds from the seeds that produce weeds, which seek to debilitate us, we will offset the vision of our mission and be enslaved by the manacles of deception. In the book, *As A Man Thinketh,* the author James Allen compares the mind of humanity to a garden. Allen states, "Just as a gardener cultivates his plot, keeping it free from weeds, so a man may tend the garden of his mind, weeding out all the wrong and impure thoughts." The expansiveness of this incredible aphorism, compels us to be the gardeners of our minds, in order to dispense of the idiosyncratic negativity in our minds, which will in turn redirect our lives towards a positive progression. The mind will produce whatever is planted inside of it, and that's why it's important to guard our thought process. There are so many distractions that come to our minds on a daily basis, but we must block out negative thoughts and allow positive thoughts to enter our minds. Whatever you allow your mind to meditate on, will eventually manifest in your actions. A banana tree will only produce bananas and never produce apples, because the seed that yields bananas was planted in the ground. The yield of the harvest is only an indication of what was planted in the field. The thoughts of doubt produce doubt, thoughts of hate produce hate, thoughts of faith produce faith, and thoughts of love produce love. The root of your fruit is only an expression of the seeds in your mind. Your mind and your mission are intrinsically interconnected and whatever impacts one will impact the other. Our thoughts are extremely important, because as we think therefore we become. If I think positive, my actions will be positive and if I think negative I will act negatively. We have a tendency to say to a person, in a vociferous manner, who does something totally obscure, "What were you thinking, or what in the world was going through your head?" Yet, we fail to realize that the action was only a reaction to the person's mode of thinking. You've got to gird your mind, guard your mind, and God will guide you to your goal. It is here then that we must eradicate the disharmony within our souls. We can never be validated or complete on the outside, if we aren't validated or complete on the inside. In this, God has come to resurrect and redirect the scope of our minds and flush out the garbage of the past, in order for us to discover the grandiose gold mine in our minds that will perfect our future. If you're going to unlock the doors of greatness that will propel you along your mission in this world, then your mind must be focused on greatness. For every distraction, there is a reaction that must be above that which seeks to bring you below. As the world turns each day, you've got to have sharp reflexes of reason, that will stimulate and expand the parameters of your mind, in order to live an ever-abounding life. I had to immerse all of the power in my mind, to overcome the Cancer eating cells that sought to destroy me from the inside out. I had to infuse my mind, with the power of the Word of God. Hebrews 4:12 states, "For the Word of God is quick, powerful and sharper than a two-edged sword, piercing even to the division of soul and spirit, and of joints and marrow, and is a discerner of the thoughts and intents of the heart." I had to purify my mind by God's Word and feed my mind positive, uplifting, and powerful words, in order to transform my thoughts and eradicate the old way of thinking in order to overcome. The Bible compels us in Romans 12:2,

"Be not conformed to this world: but be transformed by the renewing of your mind, that you may prove what is that good and acceptable and perfect will of God." The confirmation of your growth and the development of your character, is immersed in the transformation of your mind. Our mind controls the matters of our lives and will be the proponent, in shaping our mission in life. In order for us to put off and negate the old ways of living, old mistakes, and old mindsets, we must be renewed in the spirit of our minds and then put on the new creation, which is ordained of God, (Ephesians 4:22-24). The only way to move from old to new, is to renew our minds by the Word of God. The beauty of living, is that God has given your mind the power to be infused into your mission. You've got power in your mind, so elevate your dreams, elevate you vision, because if you can believe it, you can conceive it, and if you can conceive it, then I know you can achieve it. The conception of direction, is in your progression. Your progression isn't in your profession, but it's in your confession. You weren't designed to conform or capitulate, but you were designed to conquer. Each time that you offset the vision of your mission, you stifle the power of your conviction. However, you don't have to possess the nobility, because God will orchestrate your mobility, in order to maximize your ability. For where the world avoided you, God has appointed you. The place where individuals maligned you, God has assigned you. As an individual, you must realize that you are a conduit of power that can impact minds in perilous times. You might be in a predicament that's made you feel powerless, you might feel that the controls of life are dictating your progress, or you may even think that road you're traversing is far away from your visions of yesteryear. Yet, despite your supposed opposition and despite the setbacks, the darkest hour of your struggle can be transformed into the brightest hour of your victory. For God has given us interior resources, in order to confront the exterior trials and difficulties of life. This is your time to shine, this is your hour of power, this is your season of reason, this is your day to convey, this is your time to move and stretch your hands towards heaven, because your help comes from God. Every time you lift your hands, God will lift you above your circumstances. He's lifting you even now above the economic and social inequities, Christ is lifting you above the addictions, Christ is lifting you above the afflictions, and Christ is lifting you above the conditions that seem to shackle your mobility in life. God's designations of your life are greater than the situations in your life. Keep moving in God's power. Open your mind to the splendiferous magnitude of ever-abounding blessings, and march with the vision to pursue your mission. Your mission is possible because you are called according to God's purpose, (Romans 8:28). Whether people laugh at you or whisper behind your back, keep on moving forward. God's granted you the power to pursue your passion. Let nothing separate you from your vision, but pursue it with every fiber of your being. Maintain your zeal, hold fast to your ardent vigor, guard your mind, keep God's Word in your heart, and impact others with the power of your testimony as you pursue your mission. Don't look for others to give you, that which is already inside of you, but multiply your gifts because they will make room for you and bring you towards the level of greatness, (Proverbs 18:16). Everything you need is contained in the bosom of your spirit. In you is the intellectual fortitude, in you resides the creative abilities, in you is God's power to overcome negativity, in you is the power to persevere beyond all obstacles, in you is the greatness that our world is in search of to be revealed. The power is in your mind, your spirit, and it's in your hands. God has anointed the work of your hands, in order to possess the land. You have power in your hands, success is in your hands, prosperity is in your hands, creativity is in your hands, and craftsmanship is in your hands. Do something positive with your hands. The world needs your hands to make a change for the betterment of others. Don't close up the gift and power in your hands, but use your hands to esteem others. Use your hands to uplift, heal, and mold the lives of others. Ecclesiastes 9:10 declares, "Whatever your hand finds to do, do it with your might." While you're alive and equipped with the ebullient activity of your mind, use the hands that God has created to infuse value and wisdom in every arena of life that you find yourself in. The time for procrastination is over and the time for progression is now. Hebrews 12:1, 2 compels us to lay aside every weight and the sin, which easily ensnares us, and fix our eyes on Jesus, who is the finisher of our lives. No matter what it is, if it's weighing you down, you've got to lay it down. Your mission is too magnanimous, for you to live beneath your privilege. This is your time to esteem others, this is your time to exercise the power in your spirit, this is your time to focus your mind on the positive, and this is your time to forge ahead into the beauty, splendor, and radiance of your mission that God has birthed within your soul.

Chapter Seven

YOU ARE A RESTORER OF THE BRETHREN

Galatians 6:1 states, "Brothers, if someone is caught in a sin, you who are spiritual should restore him gently. But watch yourself, or you also may be tempted." The story of Cain and Abel, which can be found in Genesis 4:1-12, is a familiar story, yet it is entrenched in anger, jealousy, envy, competition, and ultimately murder. We don't necessarily know how effective Adam and Eve were as parents. We don't know what family vacations that Mr. Adam and Mrs. Eve took their beloved children out on, but we do know, within this cannon of scripture, that Cain and Abel were not reared as lazy boys. These children were born after the fall of mankind, as sin entered into the world, because of the disobedience of Adam and Eve. Therefore Adam and Eve were sent out of the garden, to work the ground from which man was taken. Adam and Eve once relished in the pristine paradise of the Garden of Eden, yet were now dealing with cultivating a garden, that produced weeds around the seeds that were planted. I reckon to propose that Cain and Abel didn't grow up with a silver spoon in their mouths, and it might not have even been stainless steel. These boys were tending the fields, cattle, and tilling the ground. The first three chapters of Genesis sets the stage for human history and the fourth chapter begins to play it out. This chapter introduces the first childbirth, the first formal worship, the first division of labor, the first signs of culture, and ultimately the first murder. In my study and analysis of Genesis, I have wondered, when did Cain turn on Abel, was his anger against his brother built up over time, and was his murder of Abel pre-meditated? When it came time to present the offerings to God, Cain was not what you would call a "cheerful giver." His attitude towards the offering and his brother, was totally unethical. So, by the time Cain decided to kill his brother, it was already justified because he destroyed him internally before he committed the act externally. Rather than strengthening his brother, Cain destroyed his brother. Rather than being compelled by his brother's worship, he competed for validation from God. The denigration and degradation of men in society, rings loud and clear. Yet, the resounding question of, "Am I my brother's keeper?," continues to reverberate as an echo in the caves of calamity and conundrums of our world. The voices of the abused are crying out, the voices of the gang-bangers are crying out through bloodshed, the voices of wayward young women are screaming for their fathers, the voices of addiction are crying out for freedom. No longer can we turn our backs on our world, in a state of denial, with a low-down, denigrated, desecrated, and destructive spirit of Cain. Now is the time, to take Responsibility as Men, Reconcile ourselves to our God, Reconcile ourselves to each other, and Restore the lives of our brothers. If God has restored your life, then He's equipped you with the power to restore your brother. It is critical for us to understand, especially as men, that we are responsible for one another, through brotherly love. The theme of Brotherhood, emerges early in the scriptures, and even later in the New Testament, through Paul's letter in the sixth chapter of Galatians. From the very beginning, it is clear that God places a high priority, on how brothers treat each other. Cain asked, "Am I my brother's keeper?" The word used for "keeper" in the Hebrew is *shamar,* which means to guard, protect, to attend, or to regard. Yet, the question today is are we responsible for our brothers? I believe God would respond with an emphatic, "Yes, we are responsible for our brothers." Not only are we our brother's keeper, but we are also held accountable for our treatment of and our ways of relating to our brothers, whether blood or spiritual. The issue of responsibility still hits home and is personalized, because if many of you were like me, you grew up in a single-parent home, where your mom played the role of both mother and father. I can say, Daddy was in the house for a period of time, but when he was there, he wasn't there. Have I lost you? I hope you understand the statement. When he was present bodily, his positive and spiritual influence was absent. So, for a twelve-year-old boy, having to witness and endure the absence of his father from the household, can ultimately leave scars on a child, who's searching to find his identity in society. So, like many fatherless young men today, I looked for a father figure on the television screen, yet athletes and actors couldn't fill the void. I tried to cover the tears through friends and the game of basketball, looking to Michael Jordan as a television type of father figure. Yes, Air Jordan could soar beyond the stratosphere, yet the apex of his aerial artistry couldn't soothe my apathy, calm my fears, or wipe away the tears. Many of us are asking, "How can I be responsible, if I never saw it exemplified in a man?" Now, as the father is ejected from the mother and the children's lives, it leaves a feeling of being rejected in their lives. So, now the children have to appropriate the rejection in many forms, whether it be psychologically, emotionally, or spiritually. Now, everyone's acting out, because all we know is hurt, so it begins to replicate in the following generations, physical or verbal abuse, and irresponsibility. Oh, we as men love to plant the seed, yet tending the soil, is where we have our hang ups. Some of the abuse at the hands of others, is replicated into sexual promiscuity, our minds are caught in a psychological conundrum, because of the mistakes that our forefathers have replicated in our lives. But I can say, like David that when my father forsook me, then the Lord raised me up, (Psalm 27:10) and God is raising you up above your circumstances or previous experiences. Oh yes, living as a man today is awfully challenging, and those who have a particular darker melanin concentration have to deal with higher hurdles. But even from the onset of conception, we internalize traits by which we are taught to parade our masculinity, and its humorous, because we say in our deep vibrato, "Oh yeah I'm a man." We speak, as if we came into this world, so hard and tough, that when the doctor slapped us on our behinds, we didn't even cry, because we don't have any tear ducts. We often think, our power is portrayed in our physical array and display of splendor, but true power is not what we have on the outside, but its contained on the inside. For greater is He, that's within you and I, than that which is contained in the world (I John 4:4). You might say it's tight, but I know it's going to be all right. As men, some of us aren't expressive at all, we're so "tight-lipped" that the only thing you can get out of us is, "Yo' man or what's up." My response is, what's up with that? God created you to be an expressive being and there's no need, to repress the cognitive power or creative intelligence that is birthed inside of you. We often place the caution tape around ourselves that reads, "Please do not cross," but it's to our advantage and the ultimate benefit of others, that we begin to open up ourselves, and we should open up first to God and the magnanimity of His blessings. Our masculinity or machismo is not contained in a list or number of women, for sexual adventures do not quantify or qualify us among our brothers, because Romans 12:1 implores and urges us to "Present our bodies as a living sacrifice, holy, and acceptable unto God which is our reasonable service." Our bodies are the temples of the Holy Ghost and God only sets up residence, in a clean temple. No longer can we smoke our lives away. No longer can we drink our lives away. No longer can we engage in illicit acts and illegal behavior, that diminishes our lives. No longer can we destroy each other's lives through violence and crime. No longer can we berate our sisters, or call them anything but a child of God. Now is the time to improve the impoverished areas of every facet of life, and it begins in the lives of men.

It is here then, that God seeks to align and direct our passions as men. He desires to use passionate men, but those passions must be directed towards God. As men, we are invigorated internally with intensity and desire. The very nature of sports, displays men who possess these characteristics, which even propels them to do exploits on the gridirons or courts, even when injured. Our passions can propel us to power, yet at the same time, plummet us to a state of pity. Our passions are often triggered by sensations, because the world caters to fulfilling, tantalizing, and tickling each of our five senses. You might possess an innate competitive drive, but the world knows how to hook you, so that you seek to maintain an idealized status or gamble your life away. You might have a passionate drive, that's pricked by the sharp and voluptuous physique of a woman. Yes, she may very well possess the measurements, "36-24-36." So, when she moves, she grooves, and when the sun illuminates the shade of her pulchritude, it rocks the very fibers of your being. However, albeit the grandeur of her display, you must remain alert and vigilant, because the enemy desires to sift you as wheat, (Luke 22:31, I Peter 5:8, 9). Don't be so impressed by the outside, that you repress your gifts on the inside. Yet, amidst the circumstances, you don't need a mannequin but you need a miracle woman. A mannequin is dressed to impress on the outside, but has nothing on the inside. On the contrary, a miracle woman has the total package, of God, on the inside and the radiant handcrafted beauty of God, on the outside. A miracle woman is interested in you, for who you are, rather than for what you have. Some individuals have a filet mignon appetite, but a filet of fish attitude (mentality). Yet, forget the hocus pocus and focus, focus on God's restoration in your life and don't let your visual acuity present an opportunity, that will bring disunity in the bosom of your soul. God is trying to take us from where we are, to where He wants us to be, but He's trying to use each of us individually, to help us get there collectively. If you use my shoulders to propel you over the wall, don't just go on with your life and leave me hanging, but turn around and stretch your hands back down to help me, in order so that I may rise above that same wall. This is the vision of today, that will resurrect the lives of tomorrow. This is why Paul emphasized to the brothers in I Corinthians 1:10 that there be no divisions among us and that we be perfectly united, in mind and thought. We must uplift each other with the power in our hands, but we don't often do that in this individualistic society in America. For capitalism is the name of the game, and it often declares, "If I can capitalize on whoever, whenever, and however, that's fine with me." Capitalism has infused its presence into the urban sectors of our country, where cigarettes, alcohol, drugs, and guns are at the disposal of young people, in efforts to wipe them out. Capitalism resides in the casinos, that strip individuals of their dignity and weekly dues. The name of capitalism rings loud and is audibly clear, as buildings for sexual entertainment are constructed on the corners of cities, in order to pervert men's minds. Capitalism has infiltrated our televisions through materialism, greed, and commercials that solicit sexuality through the various means of pitching laundry detergent or a chic car, all in the name of the almighty dollar. Our young men today have adopted that same phrase. We we're once killing each others self-esteem, with sticks and stones while "playing the dozens." Now we're killing lives with guns and knives, "flossing and glossing" on the outside, yet living in a prison without bars on the inside. Now is the time, for a change that will reverberate across the hills, valleys, cities, and alleys of America. Now is the time, for men of valor to stand up and rekindle the flame, that was extinguished in the vexed hearts of men. Now is the time, to take back what the devil stole. Now is the time, to come together, because you are my brother in the bond. An individual once said, "No man is an island," and brothers we've been working on our own too long, but if we come together, I believe things will be better. You've got the power to radically, redirect your community. If we as men join forces in our homes, communities, school districts, churches, neighborhoods, etc., there is nothing that can't be accomplished. For too long, we've placed the burden on women and they've carried us as far as they can, but now brothers, its time to direct our focus towards heaven and redirect our world positively. Paul writes to Timothy his brother in Christ and declares, "I desire therefore that men pray everywhere, lifting up holy hands without anger or disputing (I Timothy 2:1-8)." The Apostle Paul also makes a poignant plea, in the sixth chapter of Galatians, to restore the brothers that are lost. You may be saved, sanctified, and filled with the Holy Ghost, but don't parade around with a self-righteousness or sanctimonious attitude. I'm sure you can say that you weren't always living for God and your life was immersed in sin, but now that you're delivered, don't just wipe off your old dirt and go about your business, but help somebody else get their life together. Your brothers around you are crying out for deliverance, your brother is struggling to maintain his chastity, another brother is dealing with the pressures of the enemy, another brother is wayward, and in a backslidden condition. We are in need of brothers with spiritual discernment, who can probe into the hearts of the confused, misused, and abused. We are in need of brothers, that will open up their arms to the lost and love them with the *agape,* love of God. Man, since you've got yourself together, help me get myself together. I know you've been blessed, help me get my blessing. I know you've received your breakthrough, help me get mine. I know you've been restored, now lead me to restoration. For, you are my brother, we might not be biologically joined, but we're joined together spiritually. Paul goes on, but cautions us through the restoration of others, not to be haughty or high-minded, as if we've matriculated to a higher echelon of nobility. For if we begin to put our heads in the clouds, we'll find ourselves caught in the same mess that preceded our deliverance. In I Corinthians 10:12, it declares, "Let him who thinks he stands take heed lest he fall." Paul gives a stern warning against independent self-confidence, of one's moral security. No matter how serene or stable life seems, don't get lackadaisical and become so secure of yourself, but remain vigilant and soberly minded. Paul goes a step further and encourages us, not to compare ourselves with each other, and sometimes as men that's our greatest malady, between each other, because we're so competitive towards one another. Yet, in II Corinthians 10:12, it implores us that when we compare ourselves with one another we are not wise. Out of six billion people on this planet, it is unbelievably remarkable to me that there isn't a second you, anywhere to be found. You can search high and low, far and wide, but God only created you do to the work that He ordained you to complete. God's commissioned you for a work to *complete,* but don't waste your time trying to *compete.* I hope you understand it, because the enormity of His call on your life is so expansive, that the Psalmist declared, "I am fearfully and wonderfully made (Psalm 139:14)."

The disciples once asked Jesus, "Who is the greatest among us (Luke 22:24)?" We often try to validate ourselves, in comparison of where we rank against one another. It's ingrained in the sports arena, but its evident in society. Yet, Jesus replied, "The greatest among us is the one who serves." The greatest isn't the one who's adorned, idolized, or credited with a status of nobility, for true greatness is the underlying demarcation that infuses power into the lives of others, by our service to others. Enrich the lives of others with the gifts that God has bestowed unto you. Enrich your brother's life with the power that you've exhibited, in your time of perseverance. You are here to help and not to harm, you are here to esteem and redeem the lost at any cost. You are a restorer, because you are made in the image of the Most High God.

The Greek transliteration for the word restore is *katartizo*, which was used in the secular Greek for setting broken bones. The word means to mend, to put back together, to retrieve, and to reverse. In Luke 4:14-19, Jesus returns in the power of the spirit after being tempted by the devil and declares, "The spirit of the Lord is upon *Me* because He has anointed *Me* to preach the gospel to the poor, He's sent *Me* to heal the brokenhearted, to preach deliverance to the captives, recovery of sight to the blind, set at liberty them that are bruised and preach the acceptable year of the Lord." Not only did Jesus claim that He is the Messiah, but Jesus also claimed that He is a restorer. The same power of restoration that Christ has, is the same power that's in your spirit. Now its up to you to shake off that low self-esteem, shake of the abandonment, shake of the abuse, shake off the bitterness, shake off the negative childhood development, and tell the devil, "No longer am I one of Cain's kids, but now I'm a King's kid, because God has restored my life." I charge you my brother, with every fiber of my being, to claim your liberty in Christ, for He died and rose, so that you could live in victory. We should strive to not only be successful, but live as individuals of significance in society. I know you're battling the opposition, I know it hurts that your father wasn't there for you, I know you might be divorced, I know you've experienced abuse of all kinds, I know you've encountered racism, I know you might be incarcerated, I know your money looks funny and your change is strange, I know you're battling addictions on every side, but I decree by the power of God, for you to be free from every chain of bondage, in the name of Jesus and be who God has called you to be. The same way Jesus called and raised Lazarus from the dead, He's calling you even now in order to raise you to a higher level of victory. You may be bound, but God is here to loose you, you might be weak, but God is making you strong, "For your strength is made perfect in weakness (II Corinthians 12:9, 10)." Where are the men of honor? Our world needs you like never before. Rather than being a spectator, become an active participator in the cultivation of lives. Our world needs you to restore, resurrect, and revitalize not only your brother's life, but also the lives of women and children. You were created to be the model of God's magnitude. Take your rightful place as a man of valor and be the role model that others are looking for, be the man of strength, reconciliation, dispense the revelation of God's Word, and infuse power, wherever you trod your feet. You may have been broken, but God is here to mend your soul. The value of restoration in your brother, is not only a benefit, but also a necessity. It's necessary that men come together on one accord, for if we're divided against each other, there is no way that we'll stand. The writer declared, in Proverbs 27:17, "Iron sharpens iron so a man sharpens the countenance of another." You're sharp on the outside, but the world is in search for your inner sharpness. The world needs your inner fortitude and testimonies of trials that you've overcome. So, infuse the sharpness and vitality into your brother. You are your brother's keeper. The death of every man diminishes who you are, so let's keep our brothers alive and prosperous. The blood of the slain is crying out to God. Help nurture our young men and share your testimony by giving insight. The young men may not be your sons, but extend your hands and enrich their lives, in order to enhance our world. Today is the day to link our arms together as brothers, in spite of ethnicity or color. The maladies in our world have no color, but continue to affect everyone as a whole. So, as we're linked together, let's fight the good fight of faith. Put on your war clothes and arm your mind, for there is work to be done and there are lives that need to be rescued, from the fires of futility, and the ashes of anguish. Uplift and elevate my brother's confidence, elevate my sister's life, enhance the lives of young people, help me change our communities, and love one another, just as Christ exemplified His love for us. For your power is in your purpose, your strength is in your stability, and your restoration is in your reconciliation. You are a Royal Priesthood, you are a Man of Magnitude, you are a Son in God's Kingdom, now walk like it, talk like it, and live like it, for you are a Man of Restoration.

Chapter Eight

WHERE IS YOUR ROAR?

Proverbs 28:1 declares, "The righteous are bold as a lion." Today, as our world is facing innumerable battles that often cripple and debilitate the minds of individuals. We are yet searching for leaders of vision, individuals of quality, principles of power, and change that goes beyond the technological advancements and stirs the hearts of men and women. In our world, it seems as if the voices of change have been disquieted and silenced. It seems as if the fight for civil liberty, ethical esteem, and moral principles have seemingly come to a bitter halt. I am often perplexed internally, as I examine the status of our world. Our world has advanced beyond the scope of our imaginations. We possess the scientific vigor, and the technological ingenuity, but we lack the moral fiber that esteems value and righteousness in each individual. We live in an individualistic society, that capitalization is the name of the game, rags to riches, and quick results is how we like it. We have embraced a society, where fifteen minutes of fame can equal fifteen years of fortune, where an NBA draft can fulfill a young man's hopes and dreams, or where one talent competition can solidify you as an American Idol because this is the "American Dream." Yet, with every resonating dream, there is sometimes a repressive nightmare waiting just around the corner. The manacles of depression enslave our world, we've advanced so far, yet we are stifled by our own idiosyncratic and debilitating ways of life. Who will stand up and speak powerfully, rather than focus on popularity? Our young people are delving into the dark ways of living and engaging in self-incriminating behaviors. Young black men are being taught to portray a negative or hardcore image through music videos, media outlets, and magazines that yield false images, which are now transforming into unorthodox behavior, violence, murder, and sexual aggression. Our young black men are fed images, that its more popular to be in a maximum prison facility that will give you street credibility, than to attend a top notch IVY league institution, that will expand the parameters of your mind. The spread of AIDS/HIV is at an all time high and has now become a pan-epidemic. The various contraception's and safe-sex rhetoric has backfired in America, which has our young people immersed in promiscuity and early pregnancy. We didn't embrace or teach abstinence and self-control to its fullest extent, so now disease is running rampant in our communities. Where are the fathers that planted the seed, yet never tended the soil? The unwed mothers are in need of prenatal or health care and single parent mothers are left to raise young boys and girls on their own. The demise of the family begins with the man and has trickled down through his seed. For the invisible fathers that are in the home, but are not leading by example, now is the time to be the man that God created you to be. The untold accounts of incest, rape, verbal, physical, and sexual abuse by so-called "loved ones," has devaluated the self-concept of generations.

America is crying out from the abyss of her soul, not just for constitutional freedom or economic stability, but America is crying out for spiritual, psychological, and emotional deliverance. How long will we remain oblivious and tight-lipped, as homosexuality is being popularized, moving out of the closet into the bedroom? Our schools have now become social clubs and scenes of violence. As prayer has been ostracized and compromised, children and teenagers have in turn been victimized. Our governments, legislatures, and political influences of power have lowered our expectation levels, to where they have become isolated and insulated and aren't in touch with the societal maladies that affect our daily lives. Our environments are being polluted, diluted, extracted, and contracted. The hearts of humanity have hardened and grown cold. We have become numb to the pains of our world, only focusing on our individual passions and desires. This narcissistic and hedonistic way of life, is tangled in debauchery. For it's evident that our houses are not homes, our supposed places of safety have transformed into mourning and sadness. Where can we run for safety in a hurtful and crippling world? Everyone has their own agenda, thoughts, opinions, and methods of change, which has split us on all sides of the board. Have the United States of America become the Divided States of America? Our principles have been perverted. The scope of balance to our moral equilibrium has been offset. We have strayed from the moral ingenuity of our forefathers and mothers, to where the state of America and our world have become a microcosm of our very lives. Does the insignia on our country's money, "In God we trust," resonate within our hearts or has it become an anecdote of America's faith of yesteryear? For its money, power, and sex that we lust today, that has held our minds captive from the future of our brightest tomorrow.

Who will step out of the masses in order to save America and our world, from the crippling causes and effects in our lives? We're looking for answers, yet they have multiplied into greater problems. Our problems are increasing but our prayer life is decreasing. However, II Chronicles 7:14 still applies to our world and declares, "If My people who are called by My name will humble themselves, and pray and seek My face and turn from their wicked ways, then I will hear from heaven, and will forgive their sin and heal their land." For our neighborhoods, communities, states, country, and world to move from destitute to destined and from convicted to converted, we must seek the face of Christ to redeem our lives. No longer can we put the blame on others, but we must look within the mirror of our souls and rectify our lives. For man's inability is the prodigious platform, whereby God exemplifies His ability. The disunity of man can be the springboard, by which God can make us unified. The dark days of America can be wiped away, if we submit ourselves to the lover of our souls, Jesus Christ. We can only do so much, to get our Congress to progress and repress the distress of our economic and political stress. Yet, if our life continues to regress in the sins of our mess and we don't confess it before God, then we can never move into the light of true freedom. Aristotle the great philosophical thinker once stated, "We are what we repeatedly do." The people of America are caught in a cyclical conundrum, where we continue to repeat the mistakes of the past. We've studied and proposed various theoretical viewpoints of historical events, yet we are repeating the pains of the past and thwarting the freedoms of our future. The state of our world surpasses any other civilization, in reference to technological advancements, the dissemination of information, space travel, and medical achievements. Yet, we fall short of all of our accomplishments, when it comes to moral reasoning and ethical standards of behavior. We've placed more importance on the surface of an individual, rather than the scope of an individuals soul. The devil has deceived us and perverted our minds, to accept and embrace that which is harmful to our well-being.

I Peter 5:14 declares, "Be sober, be vigilant; because your adversary the devil walks about like a roaring lion, seeking whom he may devour." We must remain on guard, in opposition to the tricks and schemes of the enemy, because the devil is masking himself and parading as a lion, when he's smaller than locust. The enemy has been parading as a mascot, but its time to take off the outfit and reveal the perpetrator, who seeks to victimize our lives. Now is the time, to carry the flashlights of faith and expose the darkness that controls our standards of living. America is in need of bold children, teenagers, young adults, men, and women who will roar, by opening their mouth, in order to take a stand for righteousness. How long will you allow drugs to invade your community? How long will you sit on your gifts and talents? How long will you be controlled by your smallest crippling desire? How many more young people, will we allow to die because of violence? When will our homes become safe-havens of hope? When will we come together in order to save our nation? What happened to the sounds of footsteps marching for justice? Where are the churches and leaders, that will set denominational differences aside and unify to strengthen America? Our brothers are in discord with one another. As the voice of Abel's blood cried out to God, after Cain killed his brother, the voice of the blood shed that's destroying lives, is crying out in lament and weeping to God (Genesis 4:1-10). You are the hope for our nation, the magnificent power of God's creation, and the strength that is in need of manifestation. Jesus declared, "The Spirit of the Lord is upon *Me*, because He has anointed *Me* to preach the gospel, He has sent *Me* to heal the brokenhearted, to proclaim deliverance to the captives, and recovery of sight to the blind, to set at liberty those who are oppressed, and to proclaim the acceptable year of the Lord (Luke 4:18,19)."

In June of 1940, in the midst of World War II that encompassed the Battle of Great Britain, against the Hitler led German forces, Prime Minister, Winston Churchill declared this was Britain's Finest Hour. As England had its back against the wall, the troops mounted against the opposition and discovered the determination within, to vanquish the onslaughts of the German army. Even a decade after World War II ended, Churchill spoke of his role in the war and said, "Britain had the lion's heart, I just happened to be called upon to give the roar." I believe that now is America's Finest Hour, to exemplify the love and commitment, in order to change the face of our nation. We can't fight the battle against the strongholds that depreciate our country alone, but with the help of God we can mount up with wings as eagles, (Isaiah 40:31). There is a resounding call that declares to those with the heart of a lion and the determination of a champion, to roar and exercise the power within. Our lion's roar has become silenced, in the form of a cat's purr. While everything in our world is big and bold and as the enemy's hurdles are blockading our paths, we must not only roar back, but also our actions must speak louder than our words. If we commit to the fight to change the course of our country, we must see it through to the end. We can't afford to give up on our communities, we can't give up on our young people, and our elders must assume the responsibility, in order to mend the broken pieces. Just like Mephibosheth, our nation has been dropped and we've been crippled with little mobility, (II Samuel 4:4). We may have been dropped and our lives may have been damaged, but God has destined that our end will be greater than our beginning. The distracted are in need of guidance, the brokenhearted is waiting to be mended, the captive is waiting to be delivered, the spiritually blinded are in need of sight, the bruised are in need of liberty, the diseased are in need of healing, the addicted are in need of freedom, the hopeless are in need of hope, the poor is in need of enrichment, the destitute are in need of direction, the fatherless are in need of fathers. Now is not the time to be lackadaisical, pessimistic, or passive, but now is the time to be active and reclaim that which was lost and provide the balm of the Word of God to the maladies, wounds, and scars that have demoralized the value in our society. We can often be focused on the condition and the description, but God has supplied us with a prescription (Rx) for the conditions that debilitate us and He's given us the power for this very hour, in order to rehabilitate that which we encounter. Your roar must be heard wherever you are, so accept the call to take a stand for excellence. You might not have a pulpit, but you do have a platform. Your roar must be heard in your school, it must be heard on the radio, it must be heard on the television, it must be heard in the church, it must be heard at the conventions of empowerment, your roar must be heard in the ghettos, it must be heard in the suburbs, it must reverberate from the north to the south, from the east to the west, from Brazil to Bangkok, from Los Angeles to Sub-Saharan Africa, from your house to the White House, from the nations of the world to the United Nations. Your stance for freedom, deliverance, and moral empowerment across America and our would must awaken the dream of a Dr. King, with a passionate pursuit of perseverance that seeks to "Hew out of the mountain of despair a stone of hope, and transform the jangling discords of our nation into a beautiful symphony of brotherhood." Your stance must compel those to the saving power and love of the Cross of Christ in John 3:16 that declares, "For God so loved the world that He gave His only begotten Son (Jesus), that whoever believes will not perish but have everlasting life." Your stance must evoke images of determination, such as a Maya Angelou that cries, "Yet still I will rise." Your stance must be invigorated on a New Frontier, such as a John F. Kennedy that asked the question, "Ask not what America will do for you, but what together we can do for the freedom of man." Your stance must encompass the symphonic melody of a unified orchestra, but all in all, your entire stance must also incorporate the boldness and roar of a lion.

Chapter Nine

YOU ARE A STATUE OF LIBERTY

There is a profound call, which speaks to the hearts of the masses for freedom, from the societal and daily trials of life. We live in a world, where the young are dying young and where crime has become a way of life. In this world, it seems as if the only news worth telling is negative, the only way to riches is ruthlessness, and the only way to have fun is indulge in frivolous living. A world in which God created to be pure, has now recreated itself to be perverted. In Galatians 5:1, it states, "Stand fast therefore in the liberty by which Christ has made us free, and do not be entangled again with a yoke of bondage." The Apostle Paul writes about a yoke of bondage, which entangles, and he paints a picture of a captive with a noose around their neck, being led away by their captor, into an enslaved state of bondage. The enemy we cannot see with our natural eyes, has infiltrated our natural realm, through our spirit and has led many of our lives into captivity. We have allowed the devil to enslave our minds and enslave our flesh. Many of us are bound by negative childhood development, bound by abuse, scarred, and bruised by the world. Our world is in total bondage and enraptured, by the spirit of darkness. We can't see it naturally, but it's a spiritual darkness, that has in-turn manifested itself in the earthly realm. Romans 8:19 declares, "The earnest expectation of the creation eagerly waits for the revealing of the sons of God." While the world is tripping and flipping, yet thinking its blinging and flinging, flossing and glossing, our brothers and sisters are crying out behind the mask for deliverance. Now is the time, for America to take off the mask. America has hidden behind its wealth too long, yet it hasn't provided a solid well-being. The people of America have been masking themselves, we've been looking good on the outside yet hurting on the inside. It seems as if everyone is dancing at the masquerade ball. Some are masquerading by adorning themselves with fine jewelry, others are masquerading by acquiring wealth. Some are masquerading by covering themselves with exquisite apparel, and yet others are putting on a façade, that even though they laugh and smile on the outside, tears of sorrow overflows their soul on the inside. We often ornament and adorn ourselves on the outside, as if we were a Christmas tree, but were lacking on the inside, just so empty. You are more valuable, than the watch on your wrist, you're more valuable than the shoes on your feet, and you are worth more than the credit card in your purse or wallet. The world has placed its value on possessions, yet true value is immersed in the hearts of people. If your life is predicated on possessions, you'll always be reaching, but never grasping. However, if you're walking in the light of Christ, He will show you that your value is in the salvation that He's made available to you, and the gifts that He's place inside of you. It is here that I propose a question to you. If God has destroyed the yoke of bondage in our lives, why are we returning to what we've been delivered from? For example,

Purposefully Prepared to Persevere 95

if you were living in a one-room apartment but I put you in a six-bedroom mansion, would you return to the one room apartment and live there? Yet, some of us would return back to our previous state of living, even though a better life has been granted to us. An individual once said, "You can lead a camel to water, but you can't make it drink." You've been walking through the desert of life too long and now that the water of refreshing is prepared for you, don't turn away, but submerge yourself in the blessing. There's something wrong with us, if we choose curses over blessings. There's something inherently disturbing about one that chooses the darkness of despair, over the light of liberty. God has made deliverance available to you, so why stay bound and have a pity party? You ought to shake yourself and walk in the freedom of faith. Before God met you, the enemy had your life bound in every shape and form. After God saved you, He freed you from the enslavement of degradation. Now, that you're free, don't enter the revolving door of sin, but instead use the power of your freedom in Christ, to set at liberty those who are bound by the manacles of enslavement. Yet, the question is will you maximize your power or minimize it? Will you influence others, or will you cause yourself to be influenced by others? When all the other people are sexually active, will you remain pure? In the crowd of peer pressure, when they tell you to smoke what will you do? When everybody's going clubbing, will you tell them I'm going churching? The fact of the matter, is will you take a stand or will you allow somebody to stand on you? Dr. Martin Luther King, Jr., once declared, "If you don't stand for something, you'll fall for anything." Your life has been enriched beyond your wildest dreams, so that you won't fall for anything. You've been blessed beyond measure, in order not to fall prey to the parameters of the status quo. Stand for righteousness, stand for excellence, stand up and cement your ground, as a leader who symbolizes true freedom. The pervading question in our world asks, "Where have the leaders gone?" Former President Ronald Reagan once declared, "The greatest leader is not the one that does the greatest things, but one that gets the people to do the greatest things." Our actions are more transparent than our words, because I can tell who you are, by what you do. The true leaders are those who are liberated by Christ and are now His Statue of Liberty. You are a model of liberty, you are in God's display case, because you are His beacon of light. Yet, the greatest thing you can do is to impact somebody else's life. Its not about what you have, its about what you will do to help somebody as you traverse through this conundrum of life. You're too valuable to our world, to just settle and live a vain lifestyle. God has established your life as His symbolic statue of freedom, in order to forge you further. God has set you free to go forward, further, and farther than you ever conceptualized. For, if Jesus has set you free than you're free indeed, (John 8:36). My brother, my sister you have been commissioned to enrich and contribute to the well-being of others. You've endured many battles, scars, and bruises, yet you're still here. You are a survivor, because you're still standing. Don't allow abuse to debilitate you, don't allow negative experiences to devalue your confidence, but refuse to lose. Someone may have told you that you can't do it, but you can do all things through Christ, for He is your strength, (Philippians 4:13). Daddy might not have been there, but don't let your dreams die. The pieces of your life may have been scattered, but God has picked you and your pieces up and He's putting you back together even now. God is operating on your life and He's fusing your power and your personality, He's invigorating your spirit with spiritual stamina, He's molding and making you, shaking and shaping you into a symbolic Statue of Stability. You've stood the storm, you've stood the rain, you've stood the hell, and you've stood the pain. You've endured the ups and downs, yet you're still standing strong, because you are an example of freedom.

There is a Statue of Liberty, that stands in New York as America's insignia of freedom. The statue was constructed in 1875, beginning in France, then shipped to the United States. Its often been discussed that the statue, *Lady Liberty*, pays homage to a black woman. However, the title of the statue is *Liberty Enlightening the World*. It's profound to me that come what may, the Statue of Liberty remains standing.

> Floods may rise…still standing.
> Winds may blow…still standing.
> Hail Storms may come…the statue still stands.
> Rains may shower down…its still standing.
> As the heat rises…Lady Liberty still stands.

Night or day, come what may, Lady Liberty's arm is still raised, with that beacon of light illuminating the world. No matter what opposition arises, keep your arm stretch towards heaven. Don't let your arm down, but stretch it out, and hold up the light. You've got to stretch to reach your goals. The stretching may be uncomfortable, but in the end you'll reach the plateau of your purpose. The haters may come, but God will love you through it. You might be in the cold, but God will warm your spirit. You might be standing in the rain, but God will dry your tears. Someone might push you, but God will stabilize you. The psalmist encouraged us to be like a tree, planted by the rivers of water, that brings forth fruit, (Psalm 1:3). America has uprooted herself from the tree of truth and from the foundation of faith. In order for us to reclaim that, which was lost, our lives must be reclaimed and the fire of truth must be rekindled in our hearts. In order for America to change, the people of America must change. In order for us to be what we ought to be, we must forsake the ways of that which we used to be. In our world today, the power of liberation is compelling us to be steadfast, unmovable, and always abound in the work of the Lord, (I Corinthians 15:58). You are the light of the world, because God has placed the light of His Word in your bosom. Don't fall for just anything, but keep standing and hold up the light. You must enlighten the world, with the gifts and talents in your spirit. Enlighten the world, with the power that God has infused in your mind. Light up the world with your wisdom. Light up the world with your joy. Light up the world with your song. Light up the world with your ministry. Light up the world with your testimony. Light up the world in dark places. You must light up your school, light up your neighborhood, light up your community, and light up America for you have been liberated for this purpose. You've been liberated to shed light on darkness, "For where the Spirit of the Lord is, there is liberty (II Corinthians 3:17)." You are a Statue of Liberty, you are an individual that infuses tranquility into the calamitous situations of life. God has given us His Word, which is a lexicon of love, in order to bring visions of vitality to our minds, and equip individuals with power and healing that will enhance their lives. In these times of life, when storms arise amid the lakes of luxuries, without a single warning and sweep over our boats of benevolence, our hands must reside and abide as a haven of harmony and our love must be shed abroad like a lyrical lullaby. Stand up and plant your stance in Christ, take a stand and rescue lives from the fires of futility, in order to propel them to a haven of rest. Ask God to open up your mind, take the scales off your eyes, and give you discernment in this day. You are the model of freedom that America and the world are in desperate need of. Don't let your heart be troubled, for there is an urgent call to save nations and change generations. Use the liberty that Christ has showered down on you, to refresh and regenerate the lives of others.

†

THE RECLAMATION OF A NATION

How can we reclaim a nation that is bound
by the manacles of capitalism,
perversion, frustration, and degradation?
In the words of Langston Hughes, "Let America be
America again," but I propose to you
where does America begin?
From the ghettos and gangs, to our brothers locked behind
physical and psychological chains.
From teenage pregnancies to economic difficulties.
From drive-by's and chalked out crime scenes,
to sexually explicit music videos and violence on the TV's.
Have we become more technologically minded,
yet day-by-day morally slighted?
How can we reclaim a nation, when our hopes and dreams
are nestled in the hearts of young people, who are often
confused, because they've been misused and abused?
Fathers have fallen and Mothers are crawling,
to pick up the pieces that have been left behind.
Politicians are speaking and
Preachers are preaching
but is anyone reaching,
out to the lost, so that they can be found at any cost?
Where have the leaders gone that seek to uplift our society?

What happened to the sound of the feet
marching for justice?
Where is the strength that will, "Hew out of the mountain
of despair a stone of hope?"
Where is the love that will embrace the hater?
Where can America turn, when it has turned on herself
and her creator?
Yet, in order for America to be, it must begin inside
of you and me?
In order for America to be, Christ must live in our hearts
where He can invigorate spiritual liberty.
So, for all who read this decree
"Let not your heart be troubled."
For the answer to the reclamation of a nation is
found at the cross of reconciliation,
that will wipe away the tears of frustration and degradation.
So, for this to become true, it must begin inside of you.
Not just in the White House, but your house.
Not just on the Westside, but your side.
For the band of brotherhood and
the serenity of sisterhood,
must begin in your neighborhood, in order to
breakdown the walls that blockade our benevolence.
Yet, in order to rehabilitate the debilitated state
of our nation,
we must be determined, dedicated, and devoted
to uplifting humanity
and remain connected to the divine power of Christ.
For this cannot be all of me and none of thee,
For the declaration of this great nation was built upon
togetherness, freedom, and equality.

Printed in the United States
109957LV00001B/91-96/A

9 781425 910570